The Profession of Teaching

THE LIBRARY OF EDUCATION

A Project of The Center for Applied Research in Education, Inc.

G. R. Gottschalk, Director

Categories of Coverage

I	II	III
Curriculum and Teaching	Administration, Organization, and Finance	Psychology

IV	V	VI
History, Philosophy, and Social Foundations	Professional Skills	Educational Institutions

The Profession
of Teaching

T. M. STINNETT

Assistant Executive Secretary
for Professional Development & Welfare
National Education Association of the United States

1962
The Center for Applied Research in Education, Inc.
Washington, D. C.

LIBRARY OF CONGRESS
CATALOG CARD NO.: 62–18294

PRINTED IN THE UNITED STATES OF AMERICA

72531

Foreword

One of the basic truths in education is that the quality of education depends largely upon the quality of the teacher.

Whether the teacher be seated at one end of the proverbial log with the student perched at the other end—uncomfortable positions for both of them—or whether the teacher is in the best-equipped room of a most up-to-date school; whether the teacher is at work with a small group of students or is on a television screen that is seen by tens of thosuands; whether the teacher is a person or whether the "teacher" is a programmed textbook, it is unlikely that the students will get a superior education unless the teacher is superior. With good leadership and appropriate teaching aids, the teacher's effectiveness can be enhanced; but the most ingenious plans of inspired administrators and the best array of instructional devices are of little avail if the teacher is ignorant, unskilled, or indifferent.

It is only natural that we should look back nostalgically at the past. In our imaginations, we see the past as the days in which all pupils were ambitious and all teachers were great. There is no gain-saying the fact, however, that though many teachers in the past were capable and a few were even great, on the average they were not as well-prepared for teaching as are the average teachers today.

We have come to take for granted that our teachers should be college graduates and that they should also have gone on to gradu-ate studies. We assume that they are well-versed in the academic areas in which they are teaching. Of course they must understand the psychological, the sociological, and the philosophical foun-dations of education and we need hardly mention that they must be familiar, through both study and supervised practice, with the most effective ways of helping their students to learn. That these should be our routine expectations today is due, in large measure, to the efforts of Dr. T. M. Stinnett and to his leadership in the NCTEPS movement.

We are far from having achieved the millennium in education and we have not yet discovered the process by which ordinary mortals can all become great teachers. Nevertheless, we have made tremendous progress in teacher education by raising the standards for those who would be teachers, by improving the process by which we prepare teachers, and by gaining for teachers better public recognition of the importance of teaching. These gains have not been easy but they are already being reflected in better education for more students. Much has been accomplished and more remains to be done.

Dr. T. M. Stinnett has played so vital a role in improving teacher education and in raising professional standards that it is hard to think of anyone better qualified than he to discuss the profession of teaching. What he has to say is well worth hearing.

HARRY N. RIVLIN

Contents

CONTENTS

CHAPTER VI

The Preparation of Members   84

CHAPTER VII

Implications of the Future   101

Index   113

CHAPTER I

Historical Perspectives

The many specialties in teaching with their wide range of required skills and knowledge and, therefore, of degrees of preparation, and the vastly different nature of the teaching functions at the several school levels, cause some to reject the concept that teaching is a profession. Rather, this negative viewpoint holds that education with its comprehensive connotations is a profession, while teaching is simply a cluster of many separate professional groups. This monograph, as its title indicates, assumes that teaching is a profession; education, a discipline.

The emergence of teaching as a profession must necessarily be viewed within the framework of the history of all professions. It is, in a real sense, an offshoot of other professions; its discipline, education, is a derived one, drawing upon many others for its content.

One of the puzzling aspects of the professions is the comparatively few studies which have been devoted to their history. Carr-Saunders and Wilson in the Preface to their book *The Professions* have commented on the paucity of historic material on the professions as compared to that of trade unions.

> Professional Associations, on the other hand, have been almost entirely neglected; there has been no study of the historic development of professional associations or of the social, economic, and ethical problems involved. This is all the more astonishing inasmuch as the greater skill and responsibility of professional men as compared with members of trade unions render their associations far more interesting and important. Within the ranks of the professions are to be found most of those upon whose special skill the functioning of modern society depends.[1]

Although much has been written since the publication of *The Professions*, the relatively slender amount of published material of an historical and interpretive nature, especially about the professions in the United States, is noticeable.

---

[1] A. M. Carr-Saunders and P. A. Wilson, *The Professions* (Oxford: The Clarendon Press, 1933), p. iii.

1

The Meaning of Profession

Few words are so loosely used as *profession*. Almost every special-ized group, as soon as its members can claim to offer a significant service to society, begins to identify itself as a profession. What were only new occupations a few years ago are now fully recognized professions, and new professions are now emerging at an acceler-ating rate. Even within a given profession a high degree of special-ization may split it into several separate professional groups. More-over, many of the recognized professions are developing sub-professional groups which perform the less specialized skills of the profession.

The 1950 Census reported 3,813,770 professional workers in 23 professions, about 6.4 per cent of the total labor force of the nation of 59,642,990. Some idea of the rate at which professions have grown may be obtained from the facts that in 1850, professional workers constituted only 1.9 per cent of the total labor force and in 1900 only 3.8 per cent. To state the development in another way, the total working force of the United States increased 8 times be-tween 1850 and 1950, but professional workers increased 26 times.

Carr-Saunders generally avoided trying to define a profession, as his statement, "I have employed the word *profession* in the com-monly accepted sense," would seem to imply. He did say on one occasion:

> A little reflection shows that what we now call a profession emerges when a number of persons are found to be practicing a definite technique founded upon a specialized training. A profession may perhaps be defined as an occupation based upon specialized intellectual study and training, the purpose of which is to supply skilled service or advice to others for a definite fee or salary.[2]

The "fee or salary" alternative deserves emphasis, since it is often held that only fee, or free-lance, work can constitute a true profes-sion. This arises from the fact that the older professions were of this nature. The free lance, or fee, viewpoint is often used to deny that public school teaching is, or can be, a profession in the real sense.

---

[2] A. M. Carr-Saunders, *Professions: Their Organization and Place in Society,* Herbert Spencer Lecture at Oxford, May 18, 1928 (Oxford: The Clarendon Press, 1928), p. 31.

However, Carr-Saunders dismisses the mode of remuneration as of no consequence in view of the emergence of many new professions whose members are largely salaried workers.

If *profession* lacks a precise definition, the identification of criteria applicable to professions is, on the other hand, clear. Flexner[3] enumerates six criteria of professions:

1. They involve essentially intellectual operations.
2. They derive their raw materials from science and learning.
3. They work up this material to a practical and definite end.
4. They possess an educationally communicable technique.
5. They tend toward self-organization.
6. They are becoming increasingly altruistic in nature.

To the list above, Lieberman would add two criteria of great significance:

1. A broad range of autonomy for both the individual practitioners and for the occupational group as a whole; and
2. An acceptance by the practitioners of broad personal responsibility for judgments made and acts performed within the scope of professional autonomy.[4]

The distinguishing marks of a recognized profession are also easily identifiable. If Carr-Saunders is wary of defining profession, he does, however, describe the characteristics which denote the recognized ones. Intellectual competence is one, "the ability to perform all those skilled services upon which the continued functioning of modern society depends." The urge to form a professional association is another, which is simply a reflection of the normal urge of humans to band together to further common interests and to improve their abilities through the exchange of knowledge, experience, and techniques. This explains why most professions have been able to emerge with a single, over-all, all-inclusive, general association of practitioners. There are special interest associations, representing such groups within the profession, but these are typically subsidiary

---

[3] Abraham Flexner, "Is Social Work a Profession?", Proceedings of the National Conference of Charities and Corrections (The Hilmann Printing Company, 1915), pp. 576–90.

[4] Myron Lieberman, *Education as a Profession* (Englewood Cliffs, N.J.: Prentice-Hall, Inc., 1956), pp. 2–6.

groups to the main association, incidental to the main purpose of
the one association.

The motivations for forming a professional association, according
to Carr-Saunders are:

1. *The defining of a line of demarcation between qualified and
unqualified persons.* The realization by the members of a new profession that they possess a certain craft; and the desire of the better
equipped to be distinguished in the public mind from the ill-
equipped or the nonequipped by forming an association whose
membership is confined to those possessing prescribed minimum
qualifications.

In the early days professions sought to be exclusive, barring some
prospective members on artificial, arbitrary, or irrelevant considerations. This, of course, was motivated by the desire to identify an
elite in the practicing group. Although the expression of this very
human reaction still abounds in some professional groups, it is
usually found in subsidiary societies or associations, the membership of which must meet special qualification standards, such as the
College of Surgeons, the National Academy of Science, or the
National Research Council. In general, admission to the profession
is based upon the meeting of minimal standards. Thus, the professional associations have tended to become exclusive only in the
sense of barring those who cannot meet the minimum requirements.

2. *The maintenance of high standards of professional character and honorable practice.* Guaranteeing competence is not enough.
Members of professional associations are impelled to establish and
enforce standards of professional conduct. As difficult as it is to
distinguish the qualified from the unqualified, it is equally difficult
to distinguish the scrupulous from the unscrupulous practitioner.
Through their professional associations members seek, mutually, to
guarantee both competence and ethical conduct.

3. *The raising of the status of the professional group.* Every new
profession has to fight for recognition. Thus, their association becomes the medium for elevating the status of their members by fixing and enforcing standards high enough to gain public recognition
and recognition by other professions.

4. *The desire of the profession to be recognized by society as the
only one fully competent to practice its particular skill.* Throughout
the history of the medical profession, doctors have faced the compe-

tition of fringe or related groups. Only in recent times has legislation conferred upon doctors exclusive rights to exercise certain functions. The winning of exclusive functions has also been difficult for new professions. The battle to win these rights still continues for many professions, including teaching.

The Evolution of Professions

The term *profession* as used in modern society had no counterpart in the ancient world. To be sure, there existed the three classic professions—theology, law, and medicine, but the practitioners did not unite to form organized professions. "In Greece," writes Carman, "the lawyer was not a trained advocate practicing before a specially trained judge; he was the litigant's friend speaking on his behalf before the litigant's peers."[5] The medical doctor had no formal training other than as an apprentice or a practitioner of medicine. In Rome, the physician was, as a general rule, only a slave in a wealthy household; accountants, engineers, and architects were employees of the state. There were no professional associations.[6]

During the Middle Ages, the men who provided what we now think of as professional services were either members of the priesthood or members of exclusive guilds. The medieval universities arose from the influence of these guilds and became the training centers for the professions. The common organization of the universities was clustered around four faculties: the faculties of arts, theology, law, and medicine. Eventually, the professions broke away from the dominance of the church and set up their own associations, which in turn established centers of training for their membership. The Royal College of Surgeons, founded in Europe in 1518, is one example of the shift in control, although the connection with the church continued for some time.

By the end of the sixteenth century, with the exception of teaching, the professions had become secularized; that is, those pursuing

---

[5] For a definitive summary of the origin, evolution, and meaning of the professions, see Harry J. Carman, "The Historical Development of Licensing for the Professions," *The Education of Teachers: Certification,* Report of the San Diego Conference (Washington, D.C.: National Commission on Teacher Education and Professional Standards, National Education Association, 1961), pp. 145–55.

[6] See also Howard S. Becker, "The Nature of a Profession," *Education for the Professions,* Sixty-First Yearbook of the National Society for the Study of Education, Part II, Chapter II (Chicago: University of Chicago Press, 1962), pp. 27–46.

training no longer joined the holy orders; they formed their own secular guilds. Teaching, however, continued to be dominated by the church until some time after the Reformation and teachers continued to be members of the priesthood.[7] Throughout the eighteenth century, divinity, law, and physic (medicine) continued to be the recognized professions. This limited classification, which omitted surgeons, apothecaries, and teachers, was due to the fact that the professions were regarded as the occupations of gentlemen. To be a surgeon or an apothecary was not considered a fit vocation for gentlemen. Teachers were excluded because they were classified as clergymen; architects and civil servants, because they had not established professional associations.[8] Although the concept of a profession as a gentleman's special prerogative has had lingering connotations, it was short lived, giving way to the broader concept of possession of specialized intellectual techniques. Until the beginning of the eighteenth century, society required only some half-dozen such highly specialized groups. By the end of the eighteenth century, the impact of the scientific age and the Industrial Revolution had created new areas of specialized intellectual activity and the need for new professions, which then began to proliferate rapidly.

The evolution of professions in England. In 1711, Addison made reference to the "three great professions—divinity, law, and physic." But even this early, new professional groups were beginning to emerge as offshoots of the older ones. The apothecaries were beginning to perform some of the duties of doctors, and the invasion of the apothecary field by chemists and druggists began later in the eighteenth century. Samuel Pepys reported in 1665 that his wife had a tooth extracted by a "barber surgeon," but by 1838 dentistry had begun to receive recognition as a distinct profession.

The nineteenth century brought the rapid rise and recognition of a cluster of new professions. In the period 1800–1850, dentists, veterinary surgeons, engineers, and architects gained recognition as professions. A charter was issued to the Royal College of Veterinary Surgeons in 1844, and the Royal Institute of British Architects

---

[7] A. M. Carr-Saunders and P. A. Wilson, *The Professions* (Oxford: The Clarendon Press, 1933), pp. 293–94.

[8] *Ibid.*, p. 295.

was founded in 1834. The Institution of Civil Engineers was established in 1818, and the Institute of Mechanical Engineers in 1847. The Apothecaries Act, under which the apothecaries became general medical practitioners, was passed in 1815, and the medical profession was unified by the Medical Act of 1858.

The second half of the nineteenth century brought legislation to regulate the professions, which actually resulted in broadening the powers of the professions involved. The Medical Act of 1858, the Pharmacy Act of 1852, the Dental Act of 1878, and the Veterinary Act of 1881 gave legal recognition as well as regulation to these professions. This period, too, witnessed the emergence of new professional groups and their associations. Among these were the Surveyors Institute, founded in 1868; the National Union of Teachers, founded in 1870; and the Institute of Chartered Accountants, founded in 1880.

Legal Regulation of Professions

Licensure, either by the state or by voluntary private agencies, has long been associated with the evolution of professions. Basically, this is a means of protecting the public from incompetent practitioners and of protecting the competent from unfair competition. Carr-Saunders,[9] who uses the terms *registry* and *closure,* broadens the concept of the role of the state. The registry, as he defines it, refers to a listing of competent practitioners by the state, usually through licensure to practice. Closure goes a step further and legally reserves specified functions to those on the register of a given profession. The registry is an essential step toward closure, but it does not include exclusive designation of the functions of those on the register. Teaching is an example. While in the United States and elsewhere the state maintains a register of licensed teachers who are authorized to practice in the public schools, many teachers are not required to be listed on the register, nor required to hold licensure and are thus able to teach unhampered by the state. This is notably true of teachers in higher education. In

---

[9] A. M. Carr-Saunders, *Professions: Their Organization and Place in Society,* Herbert Spencer Lecture at Oxford, May 18, 1928 (Oxford: The Clarendon Press, 1928), pp. 22–25.

England, Carr-Saunders says, ". . . while training in the art of teaching and some three years' experience in teaching is demanded of those who apply for registration, a special exception is made in the case of University teachers, from whom no evidence of teaching capacity is required. It is not clear whether this is to be regarded as a compliment to that class of teacher or as a necessary concession to irremediable defects."[10]

Where closure exists, it is usually confined to a few professions, deemed vital in nature, such as medicine and law, and results in a partnership between the state and professional associations in the exercising of legal regulation. The associations are often assigned responsibility for conducting licensure examinations, largely determining the preparatory program, accrediting professional schools, and maintaining the register of specialized personnel beyond the basic general practitioner list. In the case of expelling a member from practice, the powers of the association are limited, since the member in question has the right of appeal to the courts.

In ancient times, licensure was informal and in the hands of the church. In medieval times, the universities provided both the preparation and the licensure for the professions. The license to practice was simply the university degree or diploma in the professional field. This practice still obtains largely for college and university professors.

On this point, a delegate of the Association for Higher Education, speaking against a proposed resolution before the Representative Assembly of the National Education Association, said:

> But for historical reasons, the situation is quite the reverse in higher education. The first modern university corporation was established in Paris approximately 750 years ago as a society of master teachers. This was an association of professionals. As the incorporated society of scholars, it asserted the rights of the profession to manage its own affairs; to prepare and certify all who would be admitted to its company . . . These rights and privileges have been preserved and defended for more than 700 years, and today the faculties of our colleges and universities are proud of their inherited right to manage their own promotion and certification requirements . . . The primary meaning of the bachelor's, master's, and the doctor's degrees is that of certificates to teach, and they are

---

[10] *Ibid.*, pp. 25–26.

recognized as such in the entire community of higher education today.[11]

Later, the guilds which were to become the professional associations sought to provide the training and to reserve exclusive rights to practice the professions. When the guilds began to decline, the state gradually entered the areas of preparation and licensure for the professions usually assigning the training function to the higher education institutions.

Prussia initiated the use of state examinations for physicians and lawyers in the early 1700's, which in time replaced entirely the qualifying examinations of the universities. The French Revolution brought an end temporarily to the medieval system of training and licensure in that country. Freedom of practice prevailed until public outrage over abuses forced a new set of legal controls. New professional schools were established and instituted examinations for practice. Gradually, the professional schools merged to form the modern universities, which, under state regulation, were endowed with the power to confer the right to practice. Thus, in France, the state exercises controls over both preparation and licensure through the universities. A counterpart of this practice with regard to public school teachers is found in the United States in the widespread practice (still existing in several states) of granting legal authority to state colleges and universities to issue teaching certificates to their graduates. In England, the state has been more restrained in entering the area of the preparation and licensing of members of the professions, leaving the former in most cases to the universities which are free of government control and the latter, to the professional associations. In most professions the professional associations are autonomous bodies that define training requirements, exercise the right to verify qualifications through examinations or to accept university degrees, and seek to reserve through public persuasion exclusive practice to those admitted to membership. The Inns of Court, for lawyers, and the General Medical Council, for doctors, are examples of British professional associations.

---

[11] I. N. Thut, Statement before the NEA Representative Assembly, Atlantic City, New Jersey, June 30, 1961, *Addresses and Proceedings of the Ninety-Ninth Annual Meeting Held at Atlantic City, New Jersey, June 25–June 30, 1961*, Vol. 99 (Washington, D.C.: National Education Association, 1961), p. 190.

In the United States, state concern and the regulation of the professions were slow to develop. Naturally, European concepts, especially those of England, prevailed. In the early Colonial days, because of the simplicity of society few professions were necessary. As in ancient times, the ministry, law, and medicine were recognized as the essential professions. Except for the ministry, university preparation for the professions did not exist. Carman[12] points out that eight of the first nine colleges founded in the United States were established to prepare ministers; that not until 1765 was the first medical school established (at Philadelphia), and not until 1764 was a law professorship (at William and Mary) established. The well-to-do went to European universities for training in law, medicine, and the ministry. Most others received their training by serving an apprenticeship under practitioners who had obtained European university degrees. Virginia in 1639, Massachusetts in 1649, and New York in 1665 enacted the first laws seeking to regulate the practice of medicine. The first Medical Practices Act was enacted in New Jersey, and by 1800 legislation had been enacted in 13 of the 16 states vesting authority in state medical societies to examine and license doctors. Law, on the other hand, was considered a public profession and was soon regulated by legislation. Six states (Massachusetts, New Jersey, New York, North Carolina, Pennsylvania, and Virginia) by 1800 required an examination as evidence of competence or an apprenticeship and an examination.

For teaching, legal regulation was even slower in developing. Both prescribed preparation and legal licensure for teachers were unknown during the Colonial period. After Independence and the formation of the Union, education was left to the states. Although half of the first 16 state constitutions mentioned the importance of education, these statements did not mandate the establishment of state school systems. Thus, the selection and licensing of teachers were left to local authorities, which resulted in low standards for the schools and poorly prepared teachers. The deplorable situation in the schools, the evidence of neglect, the indifference to standards,

---

[12] Harry J. Carman, "The Historical Development of Licensing for the Professions," *The Education of Teachers: Certification,* Report of the San Diego Conference (Washington, D.C.: National Commission on Teacher Education and Professional Standards, National Education Association, 1961), p. 148.

the low qualifications of teachers caused public indignation that brought reform in Massachusetts and other New England states in the 1840's. It had become clear that if the dream of a free, universal public school system was to survive, state regulations would have to impose reasonable standards. Above all, it became clear that provision had to be made for state schools for the training of teachers and that state supervision of their licensure had to be instituted. By the end of the nineteenth century, state normal schools were widespread, and some state control of teacher certification had been developed.

Although licensure was still largely in the hands of local school authorities, states had begun to enforce some minimum requirements, had established normal school graduation as one of the prerequisites, and had begun to experiment with reciprocity among states in teacher certification. After 1900, there began a gradual shift to centralization of certification in state departments of education, a shift which is now virtually complete.

The Changing Roles of Teachers in Modern Society

The role of the teacher, as that of a member of any profession, is a dual one. He is a practitioner of his specialty, and he is a member of his profession, obligated to further the ideals of the group. For teachers, the scope of each role has changed drastically in modern times. The perennial questioning of the professional status of teaching revolves about the ability of teachers to function adequately in both roles. In other words, the question is not so much whether teaching is a profession, but whether teachers can be persuaded to act as professionals. The teacher's role as a practitioner is an ancient one, since teaching in one form or another, formal or informal, has gone on throughout the history of man. His role as a member of the profession is a relatively recent one. In fact, the role is so new and has been, historically, so submerged in other specialized services to society that sheer inertia is perhaps the greatest deterrent to the realization of professional identity.

An impetus, however, toward overcoming traditional attitudes in this regard has arisen from the changes in the role of practitioners, changes which have occurred largely in this century. Revolutions in the social, economic, and family structure of our society since the beginning of World War I have decreed the necessity for successively higher levels of education for all our people. The shift from a rural to an urban population, the raising of the compulsory school attendance age to 16 years, even 18 years in some states, the elevation of the educational level of our population to nearly 12 years of school, and the desire for higher education, have created such demands for teachers that their numbers are increasing faster than the general population.

Technological developments, contributing to the employment of both parents and to the complexity of society, have transferred to the school many of the functions which the family and the home once performed. Thus, teachers have taken on new roles of importance and a larger place in the lives of children and parents and in society itself. As a result, schools and schooling have assumed a more significant meaning in society. The impacts of these forces upon teachers have been equally significant. One impact has been to give powerful impetus toward the professionalization of teaching by demanding higher levels of education and competence, and by urging teachers to move toward achieving standards comparable to other recognized professional groups.[13]

Emergence of the Teaching Profession

Teaching as an occupation is an ancient one, at least as old as law or medicine. Teaching as a profession is among the newest of the professions. The reason for the late emergence of the profession of teaching is largely due to its intimate connection with the church and the ministry. Teaching until relatively recent times was a function of the ministry. In medieval times there was no craft organization for teachers, such as existed for physicians and lawyers. Educational techniques, largely because of the close tie of teachers to the ministry, developed much more slowly than in most other professions. The ties to the church did not begin to be thrown off until the beginning of the nineteenth century, and still exist to a marked degree. The beginning of the separation of the dual role of minister and teacher marked the beginning of the ultimate emergence of teaching as a profession. The entry of the state into the

---

[13] For a detailed treatment of the changing roles of the teacher, see Lindley J. Stiles, ed., *The Teacher's Role in American Society*, Fourteenth Yearbook of the John Dewey Society (New York: Harper & Brothers, 1957), 298 pp.

establishment and support of schools gave powerful aid to the development of teaching as a profession. When the state began partially or wholly to finance schools, it began to set standards; chief among these standards were requirements which teachers had to meet in order to qualify for registry and licensure. This recognition came gradually to be based upon completion of prescribed training in a college or university and sometimes the passing of certain examinations.

Rise of Teachers' Professional Associations

Teachers' professional associations were as slow to emerge as the recognition of teaching as a profession. No organization of teachers, as we now use the term, existed during the Middle Ages, however pronounced may have been the common core of purposes of the men engaged in the practice.

The Brethren of the Common Life, founded in Europe in the latter part of the fourteenth century, is commonly credited with being the first voluntary association of teachers.[14] Other voluntary associations of teachers were formed during the Middle Ages, but these were primarily religious organizations and not professional associations in the modern sense.

In England, the College of Preceptors was established in 1846 by the head masters of the smaller endowed schools. Its purposes apparently were to provide some bases for the training and admission of secondary school teachers; later, it supported the establishment of a legal registry for such teachers. The Head Masters Conference was founded in 1869 as a sort of exclusive club.

Although many local associations of elementary school teachers existed in England before 1870, they had little influence and were merged into a National Union of Elementary Teachers in that year. The National Union of Teachers was formed in 1888 as a result of dissatisfaction with the public treatment of teachers. At first an association of elementary teachers, it has come to represent, through mergers and amalgamations, all teaching levels in the publicly supported lower schools in England.

In the United States, the forerunners of teachers' professional

---

[14] T. D. Martin, "Teachers' Organizations," *The Encyclopedia of Educational Research,* Walter S. Monroe, ed., Revised Edition (New York: The Macmillan Company, 1950), pp. 1442–46.

associations were societies formed as pressure groups to promote the establishment of public schools. Among these societies were the Pennsylvania Society for the Promotion of Public Schools, the Western Literary Institute and College of Professional Teachers, the Lyceum, the Friends of Education, and the American Association for the Advancement of Education (formed in 1849, with Horace Mann as president).[15]

Probably, the first teachers' association was the Society of Associated Teachers, founded in 1794, in New York City. The American Institute of Instruction was founded in Boston in 1830. By 1856, some 17 state education associations had been formed, and the culmination of the expansion of local, regional, and state professional associations was the National Teachers Association (now the National Education Association) formed in Philadelphia in 1857. The first state education association was organized in Alabama in 1840 but lapsed. The first states to perfect permanent organizations were Connecticut, Massachusetts, New York, and Rhode Island; these were formed in 1845. Currently, there is a state education association in every state and thousands of local associations. The names and dates of organization of associations for college personnel are listed in Chapter V.

The rise of professions and their professional organizations is shown by Carr-Saunders to be of great importance to society.

> Professionalism has its problems of organization. It has its weaknesses and its dangers. But taking all in all the growth of professionalism is one of the hopeful features of the time. The approach to problems of social conduct and social policy under the guidance of a professional tradition raises the ethical standards and widens the social outlook. There is thus reason to welcome a development of which the result will be to increase the influence of professional associations upon character, outlook, and conduct. "I hold," said Bacon, "every man a debtor to his profession from the which as men do of course seek to receive countenance and profit so ought they of duty to endeavor themselves by way of amends to be a help and ornament thereunto."[16]

[15] R. Freeman Butts and Laurence A. Cremin, *A History of Education in American Culture* (New York: Holt, Rinehart & Winston, Inc., 1953), pp. 288–89.

[16] A. M. Carr-Saunders, *Professions: Their Organization and Place in Society,* Herbert Spencer Lecture at Oxford, May 18, 1928 (Oxford: The Clarendon Press, 1928), p. 31.

BIBLIOGRAPHY

Becker, Howard S., "The Nature of a Profession," *Education for the Professions,* pp. 27–46, Sixty-First Yearbook of the National Society for the Study of Education. Chicago: University of Chicago Press, 1962.

Butts, R. Freeman and Laurence A. Cremin, *A History of Education in American Culture.* New York: Holt, Rinehart & Winston, Inc., 1953, 628 pp.

Carr-Saunders, A. M., *Professions: Their Organization and Place in Society,* p. 31, Herbert Spencer Lecture at Oxford, May 18, 1928. Oxford: The Clarendon Press, 1928.

Carr-Saunders, A. M., and P. A. Wilson, *The Professions.* Oxford: The Clarendon Press, 1933, 536 pp.

Chandler, B. J., *Education and the Teacher.* New York: Dodd, Mead & Company, 1961, 403 pp.

Cole, Luella, *The Background for College Teaching.* New York: Farrar & Rinehart, Inc., 1940, 616 pp.

Edwards, Newton, and Herman G. Richey, *The School in the American Social Order.* Boston: Houghton Mifflin Company, 1947, 880 pp.

Good, H. G., *A History of American Education.* New York: The Macmillan Company, 1956, 570 pp.

Huggett, A. J., and T. M. Stinnett, *Professional Problems of Teachers.* New York: The Macmillan Company, 1956, 468 pp.

Knight, Edgar W., *Education in the United States,* 3rd rev. ed. New York: Ginn and Company, 1951, 753 pp.

Lieberman, Myron, *Education as a Profession.* Englewood Cliffs, N.J.: Prentice-Hall, Inc., 1956, 540 pp.

————, *The Future of Public Education.* Chicago: The University of Chicago Press, 1960, 294 pp.

Mayer, Martin, *The Schools.* New York: Harper & Brothers, 1961, 446 pp.

Stanley, William O., *et al., Social Foundations of Education,* Part V, "Social Aspects of the Teaching Profession," pp. 577–624. New York: Holt, Rinehart & Winston, Inc., 1956.

Stiles, Lindley J., ed., *The Teacher's Role in American Society.* New York: Harper & Brothers, 1957, 298 pp.

Thomas, Laurence G., *et al., Perspective on Teaching.* Englewood Cliffs, N.J.: Prentice-Hall, Inc., 1961, 432 pp.

Woodruff, Asahel D., *Basic Concepts of Teaching.* San Francisco: Chandler Publishing Company, 1961, 237 pp.

CHAPTER II

Major Characteristics

The profession of teaching is commonly characterized as the largest of all professional groups in terms of the numbers engaged in it. This fact is reflected in data from the 1950 Census. Complete comparative data from the 1960 Census are not yet available, but there is little reason to assume that the relative numerical positions of the several professional groups have changed significantly. It is obvious, of course, that large increases have occurred in the membership of most occupational groups since 1950.

Numerical and Personal Factors

Size and scope. According to the 1950 Census, there were 3,813,770 persons engaged in work in 23 professions. Of this total, 1,251,683 were listed as teachers; 125,640 were listed as college presidents and teachers; and 161,307 were listed as musicians and music teachers. Thus, in 1950, almost 1,500,000 people were engaged in teaching or related work. This total number of teachers was almost one-third of all professional workers in 1950; in fact, the teaching profession was then more than twice as large as the next largest professional group (engineers).

An estimate of the total number of teachers employed in the United States at all school levels and in all types of positions, for the school year 1960–61, is as follows:

Teachers in the public elementary and secondary schools.	1,400,000
Teachers in private elementary and secondary schools.	220,000
School administrators, supervisors, consultants, researchers, and other specialists in elementary and secondary schools.	130,000
Professional personnel in higher education.	350,000
Professional staff members in professional organizations, government offices of education, and in private agencies with educational programs.	25,000
Total	2,125,000

Source: Margaret Lindsey, ed., *New Horizons in the Teaching Profession* (Washington, D.C.: National Commission on Teacher Education and Professional Standards, National Education Association, 1961), p. 5.

Table 1 reflects the number of teachers in 1960–61 employed in public and private elementary and secondary schools in the United States.

TABLE 1

TEACHERS BELOW COLLEGE LEVEL, BY AGE AND SEX: OCTOBER 1960

Age	Men	Women	Total
Under 25 years	40,000	179,000	219,000
25 to 34 years	231,000	208,000	439,000
35 to 44 years	111,000	238,000	349,000
45 to 54 years	85,000	364,000	449,000
55 years and over	46,000	220,000	266,000
Totals	513,000	1,209,000	1,722,000

Source: Bureau of the Census, U.S. Department of Commerce, *School Enrollment and Education of Young Adults and Their Fathers, October 1960*, Current Population Reports, Population Characteristics, Series P-20, No. 10 Washington, D.C.: The Bureau, July 24, 1961), Table E, p. 5.

Age, sex, and marital status. Of the total number of teachers employed below the college level (Table 1), 1,489,000 or 87 per cent are public school teachers, and 233,000 or 13 per cent are private school teachers. Among the public school teachers, there were more than twice as many women (1,013,000 or 68 per cent) as men (476,000 or 32 per cent). At the elementary public school level, the ratio of women to men was about 8 to 5. In the public high schools in 1960–61, for the first time in many years, men slightly outnumbered women. Among the private school teachers there was an even greater proportion of women—the women (196,-000 or 84 per cent) outnumbered the men (37,000 or 16 per cent) by more than 5 to 1. Contrary to the popular stereotypes, 60 per cent of the women and 80 per cent of the men teaching in the public schools were married.

As to the age characteristics, more than 40 per cent of all teachers are 45 years or over. Typically, women teachers are older than men, almost one-half of them are 45 years or over as compared to slightly more than one-fourth for the men. Sampling studies of the NEA Research Division indicate that the typical public school teacher is about 40 years of age, has completed 4.7 years of college work, and has taught school for 13 years. The typical teacher attends summer school every third year, works 45 to 50 hours a week during the school year, and receives about $5,200 a year.

TABLE 2

AGE DISTRIBUTION OF TEACHERS IN ELEMENTARY AND SECONDARY SCHOOLS,
BY PERCENTAGES, OCTOBER 1960

	ALL TEACHERS			TEACHERS IN PUBLIC SCHOOLS			TEACHERS IN PRIVATE SCHOOLS		
Age	Men	Women	Total	Men	Women	Total	Men	Women	Total
Under 25 years	7.8	14.8	12.8	8.2	15.3	13.0	2.7	12.2	10.7
25 to 34 years	45.2	17.2	25.5	45.4	17.9	26.6	40.5	13.8	18.0
35 to 44 years	21.6	19.7	20.1	21.4	17.1	18.5	24.4	33.2	31.8
45 to 54 years	16.6	30.2	26.1	16.6	31.0	26.5	16.2	25.0	23.6
55 years and over	8.8	18.1	15.5	8.4	18.7	15.4	16.2	15.8	15.9
Totals	100.0	100.0	100.0	100.0	100.0	100.0	100.0	100.0	100.0

Source: Bureau of the Census, U.S. Department of Commerce, *School Enrollment
and Education of Young Adults and Their Fathers,* Adaptation of data
in Table E, p. 5.

Normally, this means that these proportions of the two sexes will
be retiring within the next 15 to 20 years; that is, about 600,000
women and 172,000 men will reach retirement age in that span of
years. Assuming an even distribution of these retirees annually,
nearly 40,000 newly prepared teachers will be required each year,
alone, to replace them. These figures will be germane to the opportunities in teaching discussed below. The latest official data available
on college teachers is that for the school year 1957–58, which
indicated that 22.4 per cent of college staffs were women.

The NEA Research Division estimated that there were in 1960–
61 in the public school instructional staff (all professional personnel) 1,526,079 persons, of which 1,408,962 (92 per cent) were
classroom teachers, and 117,117 (8 per cent) were in the non-
teaching category (84,546 principals and supervisors, and 32,571
were other instructional personnel). Of the 1,408,962 classroom
teachers, 857,353 were elementary school teachers (61 per cent)
and 551,609 were high school teachers (39 per cent). Of the total
teachers (1,408,962) 93,917 were teaching on emergency certificates. Of the 857,353 elementary school teachers, 125,477 were
men (15 per cent) and 731,876 were women (85 per cent). Of
the 551,609 high school teachers, 285,632 (52 per cent) were men,
and 265,977 (48 per cent) were women. According to this estimate,
92 of every 100 employees in the public schools is a classroom
teacher, 8 are administrative, supervisory, and special-school-service

personnel. Of the total classroom teachers, about 4 of 10 are men, and 6 of 10 are women; 15 of each 100 elementary school teachers are men, 85 are women; of every 100 high school teachers, 52 are men, 48 are women.[1]

The extent of the enormous increases in the number of professional personnel, resulting from increased enrollments, is revealed by the year-by-year tabulations of public school personnel employed in the school years 1950–51 through 1960–61. In the former year there was a total instructional staff of 955,241; in the latter year, the total was 1,526,079, an increase of 55.3 per cent in the 11 year period.

The Range of Future Teaching Opportunities

The shortage of teachers in the United States has been chronic, and well publicized since the beginning of World War II. This shortage, plus steadily increasing enrollments at all school levels—the result of relatively high birth rates—plus the traditional lag of needed adjustments in the economic status of teachers, and the increasing demands for professional personnel by industry, indicate that employment opportunities in teaching will continue at abnormal levels for the next decade. But these opportunities need to be carefully evaluated or some unwarranted conclusions can be drawn. The stortages of (and therefore the demands for) teachers are unevenly distributed, numerically and among teaching specialties. What is the quantitative situation? First, we must examine the current situation and then consider the situation which will obtain in the decade 1960–1970. Several factors enter into such an examination among which are current and prospective school enrollments, teacher demand and supply, and increasing demands for enlarged curriculum services.

Current and projected enrollments. According to the Census Bureau, the total enrollment (ages 5–34) in 1960–61 in all types of schools in the United States was 46,260,000. By types of schools the total enrollment is distributed as follows:[2]

---

[1] National Education Association, Research Division, *Estimates of School Statistics, 1960–61,* Research Report 1960-R15 (Washington, D.C.: The Association, December 1960), 32 pp.

[2] There are several sources of estimated enrollments. These vary somewhat. The U.S. Office of Education releases estimates in August each year for the ensuing

MAJOR CHARACTERISTICS

TABLE 3

TOTAL ENROLLMENT IN ALL TYPES OF SCHOOLS IN THE
UNITED STATES IN 1960–61

School Level	—TYPE OF SCHOOL—		Total	PER CENT —ENROLLED—	
	Public	Private		Public	Private
Kindergarten-Elementary School	27,505,000	4,936,000	32,441,000	84.8	15.2
High School	9,215,000	1,034,000	10,249,000	89.9	10.1
College	2,307,000	1,263,000	3,570,000	64.6	35.4
Totals	39,027,000	7,233,000	46,260,000	84.4	15.6

Source: Bureau of the Census, U.S. Department of Commerce, *School Enrollment and Education of Young Adults and Their Fathers,* Adaptation of data in Table 6, p. 13.

Estimated enrollments as projected by the Office of Education, U.S. Department of Health, Education, and Welfare, for 1970 (school year 1969–70) are as follows: public elementary schools (kindergarten through grade 8), 31,927,000; public high schools (grades 9 through 12), 12,395,000; total public schools, 44,322,-000. For nonpublic elementary schools the projected enrollments are 7,870,000; for nonpublic high schools, 1,849,000; for a total enrollment of 9,719,000. The combined totals for both public and nonpublic schools are: elementary, 39,797,000; high school, 14,244,000. The total projected enrollment for all elementary and secondary schools is 54,041,000. The projected enrollment in colleges and universities, for the school year 1969–70, is 6,443,000. The estimated total for all school enrollments in 1969–70 is 60,484,000.

Putting together several estimates of enrollments between 1960 and 1970 indicates increases about as follows: Public school enrollments will increase by about 7,000,000. Private school enrollments will increase by about 3,750,000. Enrollments in higher education will increase by about 2,875,000. Thus, the total increase in enroll-

school year. In August 1961, the Office of Education estimates for the school year 1961–62 predicted a total enrollment in schools and colleges of 49,300,000, itemized as follows: kindergarten through grade 8, total of 34,200,000 (public schools, 28,700,000; private schools, 5,300,000; other schools, 200,000); grades 9 through 12, a total of 10,800,000 (public schools, 9,500,000; private schools, 1,200,000; and other schools, 100,000); colleges and universities, a total of 4,300,000. The NEA Research Division issues in November of each year estimates of public school enrollments for the current year.

ments in all types of schools between 1960 and 1970 will approximate 14,000,000.

Estimated future staff needs. Total estimated staff needs for 1969–70 are: public schools, 1,900,000, an increase of about 350,000; private schools, 300,000, an increase of about 80,000; higher education (teachers only), 390,500, an increase of about 117,000. The total professional staff needs of colleges and universities will probably be at least 450,000. The total estimated number of staff members which will be employed in schools and colleges in 1969–70 will approximate 2,500,000, an increase of at least 500,000 over 1960–61.

At the higher education level, it has been estimated that about 320,000 new teachers will be needed to maintain adequate staffs during the 10 year period (1959–60 to 1969–70), or an average of 32,000 for each of the 10 years—19,000 per year to replace those leaving teaching (an estimated 6 per cent annual leaving), and 13,000 per year to meet increased enrollments. For the public schools, there is an estimated current shortage of about 140,000 teachers. The demand for the next 10 years is likely to aggregate more than 2,000,000 needed new teachers for all purposes. Of this number 1,500,000 will be needed (150,000 annually on the average, figured at the estimated current leaving rate of 8.5 per cent), to replace those leaving teaching, and at least 500,000 (50,000 annually on the average) will be required for increased enrollments, to relieve overcrowding, to provide additional curriculum services, and to replace unqualified teachers. The figures indicate an annual average need for new teachers for the public schools of about 200,000 for each of the next 10 years. Something like 20,000 can be projected as the average annual need for new teachers in private schools. Thus, the projected total average annual need for new teachers for all elementary and secondary schools will approximate 220,000. To meet these needs, colleges and universities will have to increase their annual production of new teachers by at least 50 per cent, perhaps more. In 1960–61, for example, the 1,147 approved teacher education institutions turned out only 139,061 degree graduates prepared for teaching—53,634 prepared for elementary school teaching and 85,427 for high school teaching. But this total is illusory, since data from previous years indicate that only 73.5 per cent of the new supply of teachers (68 per cent of new high school teachers and 82 per cent of new elementary school teachers) actually take teaching jobs in the fall following their graduation; and the percentage is much lower for some teaching fields such as science and mathematics. Thus, it can be assumed that only about 102,000 (of the total of 139,061) newly prepared teachers in the spring of 1961 (58,000 high school and 44,000 elementary school teachers) actually took teaching jobs in the fall of 1961, whereas the schools employed about 150,000. To meet the deficiencies, the schools are, of course, employing teachers with substandard preparation. It cannot be assumed that all of the graduates who fail to take teaching jobs in the school year following their graduation are permanently lost to teaching. Many do take other employment, but many go on to graduate schools, or go into military service, and later do become teachers.

Any estimate of projected teacher needs necessarily must be put in perspective with probable future conditions. They can be based upon the following: the current leaving rate (estimated at 8.5 per cent); the current acceptance-of-teaching-jobs rate by new graduates (estimated at 73.5 per cent); and the past annual enrollment increase (1,000,000 or more for more than a decade) which is certain to continue through at least 1965. Also, these projections must be predicated upon current pupil-teacher ratios, but these are apt to be illusory also. Currently in all urban school districts, 50.4 per cent of all elementary classes have more than 30 children and 19.3 per cent have more than 35 each. The NEA Research Division has estimated that 30,000 additional elementary school teachers would have been required in the fall of 1961, to relieve overcrowding (more than 9,000,000 children in classrooms with more than 30 pupils, ranging to 45 and more) and to eliminate half-day sessions (involving 600,000 children).[3]

Uneven distribution of teacher shortages. Another significant factor in assessing the range of teaching opportunities is the unevenness of the demand and supply. To deal with the supply situation first—the annual production of elementary and secondary school teachers is out of balance. With a known ratio of about eight ele-

---

[3] National Education Association, Research Division, *Teacher Supply and Demand in Public Schools, 1961,* Research Report, 1961-R9 (Washington, D.C.: The Association, 1961), 48 pp.

mentary school to five high school teaching jobs, the 1961 crop of new teachers graduated by the colleges and universities almost exactly reverses this ratio—about five elementary school to eight high school teachers. There, also, is an imbalance in the production of teachers for certain high school fields, an underproduction notably in science, mathematics, girls' physical education, home economics, music, and art; there are also serious shortages in the special education and special-school-service areas. There appears to be an overproduction in the fields of physical education for men, social studies and in some places, in business education and English.

As to the demand—the areas and fields are indicated above in the discussion of supply. The demand for elementary school teachers will apparently continue to exceed the supply for many years. But the full impact of the high birth rate since World War II is yet to hit the high schools.

Another uneven aspect of the demand situation is the geographic one. The 1960 Census reveals loss of population in some states and phenomenal growth in others. The following states have had more than 100 per cent increases in school enrollments in the last decade: Alaska, Arizona, Florida, and Nevada, and the Pacific Coast states have had a consistent and rapid growth in enrollments. Naturally, these areas are in short supply of teachers and are having to import large numbers from the other states. Most large cities have suffered population losses in the last decade. Yet their school enrollments are up 22 per cent on the average and their suburbs have had a population increase of nearly 30 per cent.

The basic cause of the teacher shortages has been the imbalance in the age pools of our 5–17 year group (the source of elementary and secondary school enrollments) and the 18–21 year group (the college age pool which is the source from which new teachers must come). The first age group has increased drastically since World War II and has caused equally drastic increases in enrollments in the lower schools. The second group, because of the relatively low birth rates of the 1930's and 1940's, actually declined in size from 1950–55, at an annual rate of more than 100,000. This pool is now on the upgrade but it will probably be 1965 before it becomes large enough to produce college graduating classes of a size to yield an adequate crop of new teachers. The proportion of the first degree students who have prepared for teaching has increased since 1950, when it was about 27 per cent of the total number of first degree college graduates, to about 32 per cent in 1960. This proportion must be increased, or deterring factors removed and holding power increased, if the shortages are to be solved in the near future.

Specialties in the Teaching Profession

One of the marked characteristics of the profession of teaching is the great number of separate areas of specialization. It is not uncommon to find a cluster of specialized areas in other professions, but nothing like the number in teaching. Listed below are some of the major specialties to be found in the teaching profession; the list is by no means all-inclusive.

College. President, vice president, dean (several categories), provost, registrar, business manager, director of research, director of public relations, director of placement, director of alumni affairs, heads of departments, teachers (lecturer, instructor, assistant professor, associate professor, professor).

Public schools. Administration (superintendent, associate and assistant superintendent; directors of personnel, research, curriculum, guidance and counseling services; business management, and public relations; high school principal, associate and assistant principals, elementary principal, associate and assistant principals; attendance officer). Supervisory (general instructional supervisors—secondary and elementary schools; supervisors of special subjects—music, art, physical education, vocational education, special education; supervisors of academic fields—English, science and mathematics, social studies, foreign languages). Special school services (some of these are actually members of other professions; school psychologist, school dental hygienist, school doctor, school nurse, guidance counselor, librarian, child welfare and attendance officer). Teachers (elementary school—teacher in self-contained classroom, teacher of special subjects; teacher of special education—lip reading, mentally retarded, partially sighted, speech defects. Secondary school—teacher of academic subjects, special subjects; heads of departments).

In addition, there are many specialized positions on the staffs of state and national teachers organizations, state departments of education, U.S. Office of Education, and industrial and commercial concerns.

The Education of Teachers

The amount of formal education required of teachers is still below that of most other professional groups, and this is an influential factor in the comparatively low status generally accorded to teaching. The comparative figures (with 13 other professions) are given in Table 4.

TABLE 4

PLANS OF EDUCATION IN THIRTEEN PROFESSIONAL FIELDS, COVERING
FIVE YEARS OR MORE*

Field	Years of General College Education	Years of Professional Curriculum	Total College Years Required
Medicine	3	4	7
Theology	4	3	7
Dentistry	2	4	6
Hospital Administration	4	2	6
Law	3	3	6
Osteopathy	2	4	6
Social Work	4	2	6
Veterinary Medicine	2	4	6
Architecture	0	5	5
Chiropody	1	4	5
Library Science	4	1	5
Optometry	1	4	5
Public Health	4	1	5

* These are the most commonly followed plans in each field; there are variations followed by some schools in each field.

Source: Lloyd E. Blauch, ed., *Education for the Professions,* Office of Education, U.S. Department of Health, Education and Welfare (Washington, D.C.: Government Printing Office, 1955), p. 14.

The basic requirement for teachers in the elementary and secondary schools is four college years with variations below and above this level among the states, and with much less time on the professional curriculum than other professions require. For college teaching, the basic requirement ranges from five to seven years, with variations above and below, and virtually no emphasis upon the professional curriculum as such. The ideal preparation for college teachers is, of course, the completion of the doctorate (seven years of college), but fewer than half of the employed college teachers have attained this standard, and the percentage has been declining in recent years.

Obviously, the profession of teaching will not attain comparable status with the 13 professions listed above until its required preparation levels are comparable.

Selective admission. Another factor frequently judged to be an adverse one regarding professional status for teaching is the comparative lack of rigorous standards for admission to preparation. Several studies have been made of academic achievement levels of teacher education students and those preparing for other professions. Virtually all of these studies report lower achievement by the preparing teachers. North has summarized the situation as follows:

> When national samples of education students are compared with comparable samples of students in other curricular areas, they consistently fall below the liberal arts, science, and engineering groups, and most other groups as well.
>
> On the other hand, there is evidence that teacher education students in certain colleges that maintain high admission standards compare quite favorably . . . Under conditions now prevailing in the country as a whole, however, the field of education is not competing successfully with other professions in drawing the high-caliber personnel that it so urgently needs.[4]

Some General Characteristics

Mobility. There is a high degree of mobility and discontinuity of service in teaching. Few valid comparisons with other professions in these regards are available. The median teacher in 1956 had completed 13.1 years of teaching experience and 6.7 years in the system where then employed. Fully half of the teachers had taught in 3 or more different school systems. The mobility of teachers

---

[4] Robert D. North, "The Teacher Education Student: How Does He Compare Academically with Other College Students?" *The Education of Teachers: New Perspectives,* Report of the Second Bowling Green Conference (Washington, D.C.: National Commission on Teacher Education and Professional Standards, National Education Association, 1958), p. 285.

across state lines is believed to parallel closely that of the general population. On this assumption, at least 30 per cent of teachers are employed in states other than those in which they were born. Continuous service, unbroken by as much as one year, was reported by 70 per cent of the men, 72 per cent of the single women, and 32 per cent of the married women.

The high concentration of men in the age brackets below 36 is consistent with the knowledge that many young men leave teaching after a few years when family responsibilities increase. Many women teachers resign when they marry, others leave teaching when their first child is born. Many married women, however, move in and out of teaching; 26 per cent of the married women reported 2 or more breaks in service.

Role in community life. The roles of teachers as participants in community affairs vary according to the community. In general, in the smaller communities, it is more likely that teachers will fill leading roles in community organizations and activities. In large urban centers, where there is greater competition for leadership and participating roles, teachers are not so prominent in community affairs.

How valid are the criticisms that teachers are under-participants in community activities? There is little comparative data about the participation of other specific occupational groups. The NEA study of 1956 found that 86 per cent were regular voters; 93 per cent were active members in a church or at least one other community organization; 74 per cent were active in two or more organizations; and at least 50 per cent were active members of two or more organizations exclusive of the church.[5]

About 5 per cent of all public school teachers are employed in very small school districts (see Table 5), while more than 20 per cent work in districts with 1,000 or more teachers. More than three-fourths are employed in districts employing 50 or more teachers. In 1956, one-third of all public school teachers were employed in their home communities.[6]

---

[5] National Education Association, Research Division, "The Status of the American Public-School Teacher," *Research Bulletin,* XXXV, No. 1 (February 1957), pp. 57–62.

[6] *Ibid.,* p. 43.

TABLE 5

Size of District	Number of Districts	Number of Teachers	Per Cent of Teachers
1000 or More Teachers	99	287,800	22.0
200–999 Teachers	993	358,100	27.3
50–199 Teachers	3,949	375,700	28.7
10–49 Teachers	9,954	224,500	17.1
Fewer Than 10 Teachers	28,544	65,600	4.9
Totals	43,539	1,310,700	100.0

Source: National Education Association, Research Division, "Small Sample Techniques," *Research Bulletin,* XXXVIII, No. 4 (December 1960), p. 100 (Data from U.S. Bureau of the Census).

Personal and social characteristics. Ninety per cent of the teachers have completed a bachelor's degree, and more than one-fourth have master's degrees. About three-fourths of the teachers completed the major part of their preparation in publicly-supported colleges and universities.[7]

Some studies have indicated that the family backgrounds of teachers are predominantly of the lower-middle or upper-lower class backgrounds. A questionnaire study of a nationwide sample of teachers in 1956 by the NEA did not bear out the findings of these studies; the replies reflecting the occupational status of the teachers' fathers are summarized in Table 6. It appears that the proportion of teachers from lower class homes was small and that the upper-middle and upper classes were well represented.

Salary Provisions

Salary provisions for members of the teaching profession vary widely according to states, types of schools, and economic factors. In general, it may be said that definite procedures for determining salaries have been developed by school districts. Usually these procedures are published and made known to all teachers employed by the school district. The individual bargaining technique of a generation ago has given way to the development of schedules

---

[7] Unpublished data, based on NEA Research Division Teacher Opinion Poll, 1959–60.

TABLE 6

OCCUPATIONS OF TEACHERS' FATHERS

	PER CENT OF TEACHERS REPORTING IN 1956		
PATERNAL OCCUPATION	Rural	Urban	Total
Professional or semiprofessional worker	8.9	15.1	12.6
Managerial worker or self-employed	14.5	24.9	20.7
Clerical or sales worker	4.2	7.6	6.3
Farmer	48.4	20.6	31.7
Skilled or semiskilled worker	18.1	25.6	22.6
Unskilled worker	5.9	6.2	6.1

Source: National Education Association, Research Division, "The Status of the American Public-School Teacher," *Research Bulletin,* XXXV, No. 1 (February 1957), p. 43.

based on professional principles. The hired hand concept of the teachers' services has largely disappeared in favor of the professional concept. We have moved a long way from the "boarding around" practice as partial pay for services, which was prevalent in the early years of our educational history and extended even into this century. It was not until after World War I that school boards began to adopt formal salary schedules. It has been the contention of the profession that individual bargaining, which tended to beat down remuneration to the bare level of subsistence, also tended to lower the status of the profession, indeed to prevent the security of services of a professional nature.

Salary schedules for public school teachers based on the twin factors of preparation and experience developed rather rapidly after 1920. Moreover, as such schedules began to be adopted by school boards, teacher participation in their development became more and more common. Schedules in private schools and colleges tended to develop along positional classifications, with heavy emphasis on merit provisions.

Trends in salary schedules. Insofar as public school teachers' salary schedules are concerned, the trend has been for many years toward the single salary type. Although there has been recently a great public demand for merit pay schedules and much experimentation, relatively little progress has been made in this direction. By 1957, a total of 34 states had adopted minimum salary laws. They were extremely significant at the time of adoption, setting as they

did a floor for beginning salaries, but in most states current schedules have moved far out ahead of these prescribed minimums. Beginning salaries have been moving up steadily in the last decade,
as have the average salaries of the entire instructional staff. Greater
recognition is being given to college-year levels of preparation (the
typical differentiation is $300); this includes levels beyond the
master's degree, for six years of preparation, and some schedules
provide for seven years and the doctor's degree. Also, provisions for
intermediate steps (fractional years) between degree or college-
year levels are now being provided in many schedules. Fewer experience steps with larger annual increments are other discernible
trends. There is a trend toward increasing use of the supermaximum
increment by some large city districts; that is, an occasional increment for veteran teachers beyond the top of the regular schedule,
based on the objective factor of length of service. There is a definite
trend including administrative and supervisory personnel in salary
policy and schedules. And the trend toward eliminating discrimi-
natory practices based on differentials for sex, marital or family
status, and type of position, is quite pronounced.

Salary policies advocated by professional organizations. The
NEA is on record as advocating salaries for *beginning qualified*
teachers of at least $6000, ranging up to $13,000 and higher for experienced teachers. The NEA policy states that a professional
salary schedule should:

1. Be based upon preparation, teaching experience, and professional growth.
2. Provide a beginning salary adequate to attract capable young
people into the profession.
3. Include increments sufficient to double the beginning salary
within 10 years, followed by continuing salary advances.
4. Be developed cooperatively by school board members, administrators, and teachers.
5. Permit no discrimination as to grade or subject taught, resi-
dence, creed, race, sex, marital status, or number of dependents.
6. Recognize experience and advanced education, through the
doctor's degree.
7. Recognize, by appropriate salary ratios, the responsibilities of
administrators and other school personnel.
8. Be applied in actual practice.[8]

---

[8] National Education Association, *NEA Handbook for Local, State and National
Associations* (Washington, D.C.: The Association, 1961), pp. 57–58.

The American Federation of Teachers also advocates salary schedules based only on training and experience, or a single salary schedule unencumbered by merit rating.[9]

Types of Salary Schedules

There are many ways of categorizing teachers' salary schedules, but most of these can be classed as either single or merit pay schedules.

With few exceptions, all schedules are now of the single salary type or variations of it. Other names applied to these variations of the single salary schedules are preparation-experience schedules, index schedules, percentage schedules, professional growth schedules, merit pay schedules, schedules with supermaximum provisions.

The term *single schedule* came into use about 30 years ago, when separate schedules for elementary and high school teachers, for men and for women, for different types of teaching positions, were quite common. The drive to eliminate differentials based on these factors led to the development of the single type, the only differentials being based on differing levels of preparation and years of experience.

The merit salary schedule is more difficult to define. In fact, there is little agreement regarding a definition. As a general rule, a merit pay schedule is simply a single salary scale with modifications to reward those teachers judged to be performing superior service, that is, added provisions or differentials for these teachers above the regular schedule. The extra rewards are provided in several different ways: they may take the form of acceleration of increments by which some teachers reach the maximum ahead of the majority; or they make take the form of superior-service maximums by which the teacher, judged superior, gets additional increments not awarded to the others; or they may take the form of giving preferred placement on a multiple track schedule to select groups of teachers.

The preparation-experience schedule is also a single salary plan, in which the determining factors are the level (college years) of preparation and the number of years of experience. There are many

---

[9] American Federation of Teachers, *Personnel Relations for Teachers* (Chicago: The Federation, 1959), p. 28.

variations of this plan. Probably a majority of such schedules are based on the bachelor's and master's degrees with appropriate differentials for each and uniform increments for each successive year of service. In recent years, however, such schedules have tended toward expansion by providing differentials for six- and seven-year levels, and for the doctor's degree. Also, many such schedules are now providing differentials or increments for fractional years of additional preparation.

The index and percentage salary schedules are single schedules based on the bachelor's degree minimum. The differentials for additional preparation and successive increments are determined by applying an index or percentage to the base and adjusting the dollar amounts each year by multiplying the appropriate index or percentage by the base figure. These types of schedules have been growing in popularity in recent years. The following are examples of the two types:

AN INDEX SALARY SCHEDULE

Step	Bachelor's Degree	Master's Degree	Master's Plus 1 Year
1	1.00	1.10	1.20
2	1.06	1.16	1.26
3	1.12	1.22	1.32
4	1.18	1.28	1.38
5	1.24	1.34	1.44
6	1.30	1.40	1.50
7	1.36	1.46	1.56
8	1.42	1.52	1.62
9	1.48	1.58	1.68
10	1.54	1.64	1.74
11	1.60	1.70	1.80
12	—	1.75	1.85
13	—	1.80	1.90
14	—	—	1.95
15	—	—	2.00

Assuming that the bachelor's degree minimum is $4000 on the scale above, then the starting salary for the master's degree would be 1.10 times $4000 or $4400; and that for 5 years preparation would be 1.20 times $4000 or $4800. Similarly, the successive increments for years of service would be computed by multiplying the base for each level of preparation by the appropriate index.

A PERCENTAGE SALARY SCHEDULE

Years of Service	Percentage	Bachelor's Degree	Master's Degree	Six Years of Preparation	Doctor's Degree
1	100	$4500	$5000	$5500	$6000
2	105	4725	5250	5775	6300
3	110	4950	5500	6050	6600
4	120	5400	6000	6600	7200
5	125	5625	6250	6875	7500
6	130	5850	6500	7150	7800
7	135	6075	6750	7325	8100
8	140	6300	7000	7600	8400
9	145	6525	7250	7875	8700
10	150	6750	7500	8150	9000
11	155	6975	7750	8425	9300
12	160	7200	8000	8700	9600

Merit pay schedules. Although there is much sound and fury about, as the critics phrase it, "paying the teachers what they are worth (merit pay), rather than for how many college credits they have earned or for how many years they have lived (single salary pay)," merit pay schedules have not made much headway. At least this is true for public school teachers. Colleges, generally, claim to have merit schedules based on categories of positions and merit increments. Public school teachers have rather consistently and solidly opposed merit rating. Both the NEA and the AFT oppose merit pay schedules; they do not, however, oppose evaluation. The two terms are often confused. Merit rating seeks to compare teachers on some scale of values. This scale (or scales) is based on some judgment of what constitutes good teaching, and serves to set pay differentials. Rating, of course, is involved in evaluation, and can be used with or without merit pay. Evaluation, on the other hand, does not involve measuring a teacher's work in comparison to other teachers. Its purpose is to improve the teacher's performance, to discover strong and weak points, and to build upon the one and correct the other. Both rating and evaluation involve a large degree of subjective judgment by the raters. The difference is that merit rating is related to salary; evaluation is not. Its purpose is to improve instruction, and this is a crucial difference.

As a matter of fact, there is much confusion between the two terms, and more confusion regarding the difference between a merit pay schedule and a single or preparation-experience schedule.

School districts often report having a merit schedule when there is provision only for withholding increments, or a penalty clause. So-called merit pay schedules usually contain provisions for varying the salary to recognize teacher efficiency, as judged subjectively (quality of service provision); some kind of penalty provision for service judged unsatisfactory; double increments to recognize superior service (acceleration); additional increments above the maximum for superior teachers (superior-service maximums); or multiple tracks on the basis of quality of service with larger increments and higher maximums for the superior teachers (acceleration and superior-service maximum).

College salaries. In the biennial survey of salaries paid to college and university teachers, the NEA Research Division reported for the school year 1959–60 on the practices of 1,312 institutions, or 84.2 per cent of the 1,559 institutions asked to participate.[10] Based on this sample, the median salary (for a nine-month school year) for teachers of all ranks in degree granting institutions was $6711; for men the median was $6906, and for women $5865. The median salaries for all colleges and universities combined were: for professors, $9107 (one-fourth at or above $10,775, one-fourth at or below $7721); for associate professors, $7332 (one-fourth at or above $8206, one-fourth at or below $6439); for assistant professors, $6231 (one-fourth at or above $6889, one-fourth at or below $5589); for instructors, $5059 (one-fourth at or above $5624, one-fourth at or below $4599).

The range of salaries of college teachers by rank is wide; median salaries may be misleading. For example, in the institutions studied, more than 300 teaching positions carried salaries in excess of $18,000; more than 1,000 positions ranged in salary above $15,-000; 10 per cent of the positions paid salaries of $10,000 or more; and for full professors about 10 per cent received salaries at or above $13,000. The annual salaries of some college or university presidents ranged above $40,000, at least 20 receiving $30,000 or above and about 100 receiving $20,000 and above. The median is $13,827, and one-fourth receive less than $10,500.

On the dark side of the college teachers' salary picture are the

---

10 National Education Association, Research Division, *Salaries Paid and Salary Practices in Universities, Colleges and Junior Colleges, 1959–60*, Research Report 1960-R3 (Washington, D.C.: The Association, March 1960), 55 pp.

TABLE 7

COMPARISON OF MEDIAN SALARIES OF COLLEGE TEACHERS, ALL RANKS,
BY TYPE OF INSTITUTION, AND PUBLIC SCHOOL TEACHERS, 1959–60

Type of Institution	Median Salary
State Universities	$7,136
Nonpublic Universities	7,179
Municipal	8,042
Land Grant Colleges	6,984
State Colleges	6,549
Teachers Colleges	6,654
Nonpublic Colleges (over 1,000 enrollment)	6,105
Junior Colleges, public and nonpublic	6,242
Public School Classroom Teachers	5,025

Source: *Ibid.*, p. 9.

following: 14,000 received less than $5,000 and 22,000 received
between $5,000 and $6,000; the median salary of assistant professors in the small nonpublic colleges was only $4,660; and for in-
structors, who usually carry heavy teaching loads, the median salary
in all types of institutions was only $5,095.

BIBLIOGRAPHY

Bureau of the Census, "School Enrollment and Education of Young Adults
and Their Fathers," *Current Population Reports, Population Characteristics,* October 1960, Series P-20, No. 10. Washington, D.C.: The Bureau
of the Census, July 24, 1961.

Chandler, B. J., *Education and the Teacher.* New York: Dodd, Mead &
Company, 1961, 403 pp.

Good, H. G., *A History of American Education.* New York: The Macmillan
Company, 1956, 570 pp.

Knight, Edgar W., *Education in the United States,* 3rd rev. ed. New York:
Ginn and Company, 1951, 753 pp.

Lieberman, Myron, *Education as a Profession.* Englewood Cliffs, N.J.:
Prentice-Hall, Inc., 1956, 540 pp.

National Education Association, Association for Higher Education, *Compen-
sation on the Campus.* Washington, D.C.: The Association, 1961,
528 pp.

National Education Association, *Handbook for Local, State, and National
Associations,* 1961–62. Washington, D.C.: The Association, 1961,
343 pp.

National Education Association, National Commission on Teacher Education and Professional Standards, Margaret Lindsey, ed., *New Horizons in the Teaching Profession.* Washington, D.C.: The Association, 1961, 243 pp.

National Education Association, Research Division, *Why Have Merit Plans Been Abandoned?,* Research Report 1961-R15. Washington, D.C.: The Association, February 1961, 51 pp.

————, *Estimates of School Statistics, 1960–61,* Research Report 1960-R3. Washington, D.C.: The Association, December 1960, 32 pp.

————, *The Status of the American Public-School Teacher,* NEA Research Bulletin, 35:43, Washington, D.C.: The Association, February 1957, 53 pp.

————, *Teacher Supply and Demand in the Public Schools, 1961,* Research Report 1961-R9. Washington, D.C.: The Association, 48 pp. (Issued annually.)

North, Robert D., "The Teacher Education Student: How Does He Compare With Other College Students?", *The Education of Teachers: New Perspectives.* Washington, D.C.: National Commission on Teacher Education and Professional Standards, National Education Association, 1958, pp. 278–285.

CHAPTER III

Professional and Legal Status

It was pointed out in Chapter I that the profession of teaching is not yet clearly established or fully accepted. The terminology is familiar, long-imbedded in custom, and widely used in writings, but acceptance of the idea of teaching as a profession is not universally embraced even by those who practice it. And general recognition of teaching as a profession is withheld by the public, probably as much as anything else the natural concomitant of the uncertainty of its own membership. This uncertainty is pointed up by Bestor.[1]

> Educationists are morbidly self-conscious about the standing of their profession. They exhort one another to be "professional minded" and each feels his pulse from time to time to make sure that it has the right professional beat. Beneath it all, however, lies a frightened uncertainty concerning the exact nature of a profession and a desperate longing for palpable tokens of salvation.

Obstacles to the Professionalization of Teaching

Part of the uncertainty regarding professional status arises from history and tradition. The close identification with the ministry until comparatively recent times is one factor. The low economic and social status of teachers in early America is another. In some of the American colonies, the first teachers were indentured servants. Knight refers to the practice of "buying" teachers as well as slaves from incoming ships in Baltimore. In fact, the low preparation and admission requirements which had obtained since the founding of the common schools, and which still persist for public school teachers in some places, helped to implant in the public mind an image of inferiority and ineptness. Not until the educational level of teachers began to pull ahead of that of the general population did the public concept of teaching begin to change; this development has largely taken place in this century.

---

[1] Arthur Bestor, *The Restoration of Learning* (New York: Alfred A Knopf, 1955), p. 269.

Low status of elementary school teachers. Probably the greatest single obstacle to the achievement of professional status and recognition has been the inferior role accorded elementary school teachers. Traditionally, the public thought they needed to know only a little more than the little children they taught. Even the teaching profession itself accepted or acquiesced in this notion until recent years. Only in 1930, did the first state require the bachelor's degree for beginning elementary school teachers; and not until 1948 did the profession, through the National Commission on Teacher Education and Professional Standards, enunciate the policy of equal preparation standards for elementary and secondary school teachers. This policy is not yet fully operative, but it is virtually universally accepted.

Predominance of women in teaching. Another serious obstacle to the professionalization of teaching is the predominance of women in teaching positions. This has been true of all professions in which a relatively large proportion of the practitioners were women; the reason is, of course, biological and not inferior ability. The interruption of careers, or the termination of them, for child bearing and rearing and family duties, inevitably dictate an in-and-out role for women. Not only does this cause instability in the teaching staff, it creates other adverse factors. Low pay, large turnovers, a high leaving rate, pressures for mass production instead of excellence in teacher education, and indifference to professional status and growth tend to result from the predominance and impermanence of women in teaching.

Status in teaching. Still another drawback to full professional recognition for teaching is the reluctance of college and university teachers to be classed as teachers, or at least to be classified alongside the teachers in the lower schools. There are, of course, vast differences in the histories of the two groups, differences in origin, preparation, and prestige. Generally, the higher education teacher categorizes himself as a scholar, or as a mathematician, a scientist, a humanist, a historian, and not as a teacher. By regarding himself first as a professional in his subject area and only incidentally or reluctantly as a professional in teaching, the college teacher tends to create and perpetuate a gulf between himself and teachers at the lower school levels; there are even such rivalries among the various teaching fields. Status schisms between elementary and high school teachers also exist intensely in some countries and to some degree in the United States.

Legal Status of Teaching

In general, professions are regulated by law or have the sanction of law. At least this has come to be true in modern society. It is true that with respect to most professions in the United States the law tends to vest rather broad powers for self-regulation; yet the law of the respective states is the source of this power, and in a broad sense this is the regulatory authority. This is a comparatively recent development. The preparation for and the sanction to practice the professions from their origins to roughly the eighteenth century was casual and largely uncontrolled by society.

This chapter will seek to examine the extent of legal provisions applied to teachers and the extent of self-regulation granted by the law. Both will be examined in the light of comparisons to other professions.

Teaching, as is the case with virtually all professional groups, is recognized in the laws of the respective states and is regulated by these laws. The difference in the extent of regulation is one of degree. Typically, public school teaching, because it is a public profession in the sense that it is supported by taxation, is regulated more directly and in somewhat greater detail than most other professional groups.

The distinction must be made at this point between members of the profession of teaching who are employed in the public elementary and secondary schools (including those in public junior colleges and state teachers colleges in some states) on the one hand, and those employed in private elementary and secondary schools, colleges, and universities (both public and private, with the exceptions noted above) on the other. The latter categories have relatively few regulatory legal restrictions. As described below, in a few states teachers in private elementary and secondary schools are subject to some preparation standards through legal certification provisions. This is true in cases where the schools in which they are employed seek accreditation by the state. Also, most states have some specifications for chartering a college or university and some provisions regarding liability or exemption from liability. In general, however, for teachers in private schools and higher education most of the provisions in law regarding public school teachers—such as educational and personal qualifications, licensure, revocation of licensure, retirement provisions, and tenure—are left largely to the regulations of the employing schools, which in turn are governed somewhat in these matters by the standards or criteria of the accrediting bodies to which they belong.

Comparisons with Other Professions

In a study by the NEA Research Division which compared provision in the law for teaching with those for five other professions (Accounting, Architecture, Law, Medicine, and Nursing) with respect to two aspects only—certification and the revocation of certificates—it was stated:

> Teaching differs fundamentally from the other professions dealt with in this report in that teachers are public employees who can be effectively driven out of the profession by dismissal from position, as well as by revocation of license. Members of other professions can be driven out of their professions only by cancellation of their licenses. In order to give teachers the professional security and continuance in their profession, enjoyed by other professions, they need not only sound and well-guarded legal procedure for revocation of licenses but also a like procedure before positions are terminated. In other words, teachers need a dual protection, whereas the other professions considered ordinarily need only a well-guarded protection against improper revocation of license.[2]

Since the professions are regulated by the states, the matter of licensure (admission to practice) and of revocation of license (expulsion from practice) is vested in boards. Professional control over these vital matters is usually secured by control of the respective boards and by securing legislation providing that membership be made up of practicing members of the professions involved. For virtually all professions except teaching this is the case. Lieberman's analysis (from 1952 data) of the composition of these boards found that all or a majority of the membership of them except for teaching

---

[2] National Education Association, Research Division, *Statutory Status of Six Professions*, XVI, No. 4, Foreword by Donald DuShane (Washington, D.C.: The Association, September 1938), p. 184.

were members of their respective professions. The listing with the number of states providing for professional boards (numbers in parentheses refer to states for which information was not available) is as follows: Attorneys 48; Physicians 48; Dentists 48; Pharmacists 46 (2); Optometrists 46 (2); Registered Nurses 44 (1); Barbers 42 (3); Accountants 41 (5); Beauticians 38 (4); Architects 34 (6); Chiropractors 34 (4); Chiropodists 31; and Teachers 5 (1).[3]

How Extensive is Professional Autonomy?

Lieberman also states that "there is no guarantee of professional control unless the profession itself has the power either to select the board [licensing] members or at least to veto the selection of members unacceptable to it. If the members of the licensing board are selected without reference to the wishes of the profession, professional control may be lacking."[4]

This contention is borne out by a recent report on the difficulty of revoking the licensure of doctors.[5] In the public mind and in the other professions, especially among teachers, an image prevails of an all-powerful medical profession that exercises complete control over admission to and expulsion from practice. But the magazine report referred to reflects a different image, an image of frustration and impotency by the profession when it seeks to rid itself of incompetents. It is true that a local medical society can drop a colleague from the staff of a hospital and debar him from use of the hospital, but there is little control over revocation of legal license to practice. Denial of the hospital privilege, also, does not appear to be as powerful a weapon as has been assumed. The debarred doctor can continue to practice and often can find another hospital. In many cases the efforts of the medical profession to debar members from practice have resulted in libel and defamation suits, and in some instances of court suits to remove the ban. Conviction of doctors for criminal offenses or for illegal practice can be handled

---

[3] Myron Lieberman, *Education as a Profession* (Englewood Cliffs, N.J.: Prentice-Hall, Inc., 1956), p. 95.

[4] *Ibid.*, p. 95.

[5] Milton Silverman, "Can We Get Rid of Bad Doctors?", *The Saturday Evening Post*, August 5, 1961, pp. 19; 47–48.

effectively, but the separation of incompetents from practice is almost impossible. Another fallacy that makes it difficult for the medical profession to discipline its members is the popular notion that all doctors belong to their medical societies; the fact is that many doctors are not members of their city or county medical societies or of the American Medical Association. These non-members are, therefore, largely beyond the disciplining powers of the medical profession. This report concludes, in effect, that the medical profession must seek legislation empowering it to discipline its membership or the states will eventually set up their own machinery to do so.

The teaching profession faces the same basic problem as all other professions in securing even-handed justice in regard to continuation in practice. The problem of assuring admission to practice of competent people is difficult enough, but not nearly so difficult as that of safeguarding the job equity of the competent and at the same time finding effective means for separating the incompetent or the unethical from practice; a recognized profession must assume major responsibility for both. It cannot in good conscience or in good faith with the public insist upon the right to protect its members against unfair or capricious dismissal practices unless it is also willing and able to undertake the onerous task of weeding out the unethical and incompetent practitioners who, in some numbers, get admitted to practice. The teaching profession, as is true of all professions, has three weapons with which to approach this problem. The first is legal, the sanction of law. The second is those legal rights and responsibilities vested in the profession. The third is the extra-legal, voluntary machinery of the organized profession itself established specifically to protect and discipline the membership. The first is the basic law regulating the profession established to serve the interests and welfare of society. The sovereign power with respect to regulation of professions is that of the respective states through their legislatures. But this is not enough. If the sanctions are vested wholly or largely in legal agencies, as has been pointed out above in the discussion of the problems of the medical profession, it is inadequate. The law must vest some powers in the profession to establish and enforce standards for admission to practice and for continuation in practice. And the law must spell out the rights and the responsibilities of the profession and its members.

Court Cases Involving Teachers

Legal status of teachers is defined in state law, in the regulations of state education agencies, in the policies of local school boards, and in the interpretations of the courts. Since the legal functions of state and local boards are defined by state law and constitution, many cases involving teachers find their way to the state and federal courts.

Every year the NEA Research Division compiles a review of court decisions pertaining to teachers. During 1960, for example, 54 cases were reviewed, in which the litigants were teachers or other school personnel in the public schools and public colleges and universities.[6] These cases arose in 26 states and the District of Columbia. Lower state courts decided 25 of these cases; 26 were decisions of state supreme courts; 1 by a federal court; and 2 were rendered by the Supreme Court of the United States. All except one of the cases were civil actions. The exception was the case of a teacher who had been convicted for contempt of Congress for refusing on Constitutional grounds to answer questions of the House Committee on Un-American Activities. The appeal was successful.

In order of frequency, the 54 cases involved the following matters: tenure, 17 cases; contract, 7 cases; salary, retirement, and loyalty questions, 6 cases each; liability for pupil injuries, 4 cases; certification, 3 cases; miscellaneous, 8 cases.

One of the cases reaching the Supreme Court of the United States, involved two teachers who objected to a state law (Arkansas) requiring them to file affidavits listing all organizations to which they had belonged during the last five years. The Supreme Court declared the statute to be unconstitutional under the Fourteenth Amendment as a restraint on the right of freedom of association. A similar case came from the state of Washington involving a state law requiring an oath disclaiming membership or activities in subversive organizations and providing for dismissal of an employee who refuses to sign an oath. The Supreme Court remanded the case to the state court to determine whether the employee was

---

6 National Education Association, Research Division, *The Teacher's Day in Court,* Research Report 1961-R7 (Washington, D.C.: The Association, April 1961), 46 pp.

given a hearing to explain or defend his refusal to sign before dismissal.

Two cases involved dismissal of teachers, in Pennsylvania and New Jersey, for incompetency under the state teacher tenure law because of their refusal to answer questions about membership in the Communist Party before a subcommittee of the House Un-American Activities Committee. The Pennsylvania Supreme Court reversed the orders dismissing the teachers on the grounds that the teachers were deprived of due process of law in being dismissed for using the protections of the Fifth Amendment. The New Jersey Supreme Court held that the school board's inquiry of fitness to teach should deal only with present membership.

Of the retirement cases, one involved determination of a beneficiary, and the others dealt with eligibility of certain school employees to be covered by teacher retirement systems, mandatory retirement provisions, and means of computing retirement benefits.

Legal Provisions Regulating Public School Teachers

Requirements for admission.[7] In the United States, all states, the District of Columbia, and Puerto Rico (for convenience these will be referred to as the 52 states) require a legal license to be held by all professional personnel in the public schools, generally extending from grades 1 through 12. However, 14 states require public nursery school teachers to hold certificates; 40 states require teachers in kindergartens and 13 states require public junior college teachers to be certificated. Four states require teachers in state teachers colleges to have certificates. In addition, 15 states require teachers at some school levels or areas, and in some positions in private elementary and high schools to hold legal certificates. The predominant practice among states with respect to private school teachers, however, is to make legal licensure voluntary or to require such licensure only if a particular school seeks state accreditation.

Authority for certification. In virtually all states, the licensing body for teachers is the chief state education agency, either the state board of education or the state department of education (in some

---

[7] Material for this section was secured largely from W. Earl Armstrong and T. M. Stinnett, *A Manual on Certification Requirements for School Personnel in the United States,* 1961 Edition, a biennial manual issued since 1951 and published by the National Education Association, Washington, D.C.

cases it is called the state department of public instruction). In five states (Colorado, Indiana, Nebraska, North Dakota, and Puerto Rico) some considerable authority for prescribing the requirements for teachers' certificates is retained in law. In all other states almost complete authority to set requirements, issue and revoke certificates is vested in the state department of education. The law in most states granting such authority does specify a few general provisions, such as minimum age and citizenship, health, oaths, and special courses, such as state history and constitution. With few exceptions this is exclusive authority. In the following 10 states the authority of state departments of education is shared: (7 share authority with cities) Delaware (city of Wilmington); Illinois (city of Chicago); Maryland (city of Baltimore); New York (cities of Buffalo and New York); North Dakota (3 cities may issue certificates, but only 1 exercises this authority); Oregon (city of Portland); Pennsylvania (county or district superintendents are authorized to issue emergency certificates of limited duration); 4 share authority with state colleges and/or universities (Kansas, Missouri, North Dakota, and South Dakota).

Requirements for certification. In 1961, a total of 44 states enforced the minimum preparation of the bachelor's degree for beginning elementary school teachers (see Table 10). Seven states and Puerto Rico issue such certificates on less preparation. The seven states are: Arkansas, Maine, Montana, Nebraska, North Dakota, South Dakota, and Wisconsin. All states except Arkansas enforce the minimum of the bachelor's degree for high school teachers, and two states (Arizona and California) and the District of Columbia enforce five college years of preservice preparation. In addition, nine states (Arizona, California, Connecticut, Indiana, Maryland, New York, Oregon, Pennsylvania, and Washington) mandate the completion of a fifth year of college preparation for high school or elementary school teachers or both within a specified number of years of teaching on the initial teaching certificate based on the bachelor's degree. The requirements for administrative, supervisory, and special-school-service personnel are somewhat higher.

Slow development of certification standards. One of the striking features of the long struggle of teaching to become recognized as a profession has been the lag between its prescribed levels of preparation for admission to practice and those of the other professions.

Teaching is just now reaching the nearly universal enforcement of the bachelor's degree as a minimum prerequisite. All other professions have long since adopted from four to seven years of undergraduate and post graduate preparation. Also, teaching is still struggling to retain a bare legal minimum of professional preparation (typically 18 hours for high school teachers—about one-seventh of the degree program; and 24 hours for elementary school teachers—about one-sixth of the degree program; or about 24 and 30 hours—or one-sixth and one-fourth respectively of institutional minimums), whereas the other professions mandate from one to four college years of strictly professional preparation. The relative slowness with which teaching has moved toward professional levels of preparation is reflected in Table 8.

TABLE 8

NUMBER OF STATES ENFORCING THE BACHELOR'S DEGREE REQUIREMENT
FOR ELEMENTARY AND HIGH SCHOOL TEACHERS, BY DECADES

| | ——NUMBER OF STATES ENFORCING—— | |
Year	For Elementary School Teachers	For High School Teachers
1900	0	2
1910	0	3
1920	0	10
1930	2	23
1940	11	40
1950	21	42
1960	40*	51**

* Four additional states became degree states in 1961.
** Three states (Minnesota, North Dakota, and South Dakota) reported uncertainty regarding the year in which the degree requirement was instituted.

Source: W. Earl Armstrong and T. M. Stinnett, *A Manual on Certification Requirements for School Personnel in the United States,* 1961 Edition (Washington, D.C.: National Education Association, 1962), p. 10.

It is obvious from the data in Table 8 that the chief obstacle to the enforcement of degree requirements for beginning teachers has been the public attitude, perhaps widely held by teachers themselves, that a full college education was not necessary for elementary school teachers. The first known date that a state (Utah) began enforcing the degree for high school teachers was 1897, and California adopted the five-year requirement in 1905. It was not until 1930, 33 years later, that 2 states (California and the District of Columbia) inaugurated the degree requirement for elementary school teachers. By the end of World War II only about 15 states had achieved this level. In the years from 1950 to 1961, 23 states moved to the degree level because of a concerted drive to move the concept of elementary school teaching to the same level of importance as that of high school teachers.

Examination as a part of teacher certification. Examinations are closely tied in with admission to most professions. These are qualifying examinations superimposed upon the required number of years of college preparation. In teaching such examinations are rare, but do exist. South Carolina uses the National Teachers Examination (NTE) to qualify teachers after college graduation for a particular grade of initial certificate—A, B, C, or D (geared to a prescribed salary schedule)—and to permit certified teachers to qualify for additional teaching fields or subjects in the high school. West Virginia uses the NTE to qualify liberal arts college graduates for provisional certificates. The District of Columbia requires a qualifying examination of all candidates for certification and employment in addition to the degree requirements. Illinois will certificate elementary school teachers on the basis of a qualifying examination if they have completed two years of college work. Several states use the proficiency examinations to qualify candidates for certain types of positions if they already possess a teaching certificate or have completed the prescribed college work. Georgia requires passage of NTE in addition to six years of college preparation for its six-year certificate. The Florida Legislature has decreed (effective in the school year 1962–63) the use of the NTE or the Graduate Record Examination for initial certification and to determine merit salary awards for a prescribed proportion of the teachers in each county. Hawaii and Maine require an examination in addition to prescribed college preparation for administrative certificates. Several of the states requiring a special course, such as state history, accept the passage of an examination in the subject in lieu of completing a formal credit course.

Number of teachers' certificates. A chief mark of professions other than teaching is the issuance of only one legal license to all practitioners—a license authorizing the holder to practice the profession. Certification of competence in a particular area of specialization is vested in the professional association, which prescribes additional preparation and a qualifying examination for a certificate of competence.

Teaching has not as yet attained this unification. The states issue a total of 579 separately named teaching certificates; the median number issued by the states is 9, with the range being from 2 to 68.

Critics point to this extraordinary proliferation of certificates as a prime reason why teaching is not recognized as a profession. Each specialized group as it emerges insists upon a separate certificate, hoping thereby to exclude the unqualified and to gain special status for the specialization. This practice, say the critics, tends to fragment teaching into many separate professions. The National Commission on Teacher Education and Professional Standards has recommended one basic teaching credential, with endorsement of specialties and the gradual assumption of the right to certify specialties with preparation requirements beyond the basic teaching credential by professional associations. A slight trend in this direction is now beginning to emerge.

Restrictive Employment Provisions

All states have legal specifications regarding procedures and conditions of employment of teachers. Qualifying for a legal certificate is only evidence that the state's minimum requirements have been met, and it authorizes the holder to seek employment. School boards, generally, are vested with authority to specify additional qualifications, and there are usually restrictions in the law which prohibit boards from employing certain teachers, although such teachers may have been issued a certificate by the state.

Ordinarily, the school board is the legal employing agency. In some states boards have the authority to delegate this power to the superintendent. And some state laws prescribe that the board employment of teachers must follow nominations of the superintendent.

In 22 states,[8] there are anti-nepotism provisions prohibiting the employment of teachers who are relatives of members of the school board. These laws vary somewhat with regard to the degree of relationship and the specifications of certain exceptions. In 6 of the

---

[8] Arizona, Arkansas, Florida, Idaho, Kansas, Minnesota, Mississippi, Missouri, Montana, Nebraska, Nevada, New York, North Dakota, Ohio, Oklahoma, Oregon, Pennsylvania, South Carolina, South Dakota, Texas, Utah, Virginia.

states, such teachers may be employed by unanimous vote of the board; one state permits employment of a relative if two-thirds of the qualified electors of the district vote for his employment; in another state a relative may be employed if 50 per cent of the electors in the district sign a petition approving the employment. These provisions do not apply to a teacher already employed by a school district when a relative is elected to the board. In 6 states (Illinois, Massachusetts, Missouri, New Jersey, New York, and Pennsylvania) and in the District of Columbia school boards require or authorize the appointment of teachers from eligibility lists derived from results of examinations administered to candidates. These state laws are not state-wide, usually applying only to certain cities. In addition, many cities have established rules and procedures for selecting teachers, including the use of examinations, even though there is no specific grant of authority in the law to do so.

Quite common a generation ago were laws or local board regulations requiring teachers to be citizens of the state or residents of the employing community. Although a few of these requirements remain in force, the trend is quite definitely toward dropping them.

In 33 states, there are requirements that teachers sign an oath to support the Constitution of the United States and (in most cases) the constitution of the state. An oath to refrain from membership in subversive groups is required in 14 states; and 10 other states have statutes prohibiting membership in subversive groups. Probably as a result of the Federal Hatch Act, passed in 1939, many states have enacted laws defining restrictions and rights of teachers to engage in political activities.

Protective Employment Provisions in Statutes

All states but 3 (Utah, Vermont, and Wyoming) have legislation regarding teachers' contracts and their terms. Not all teachers in the states having such legislation are covered. While 32 states have legislation providing for tenure and tenure-type continuing contracts, only 25 have legislation state-wide in nature, and seven states have laws applicable only in certain places. There are some deviations in a few of the so-called state-wide laws. In addition, 12 states have state-wide continuing contract laws, of which 7 are of the limited tenure scope and 5 are of the spring-notification type.

Thus, there are 44 states that provide some legal job protection of teachers by law.

A tenure law or continuing contract law of the tenure type specifies that before dismissal of a teacher, either during or at the close of the school year, the teacher must receive notice, a statement of the charges, and a hearing. A straight continuing contract law simply provides that the contract is in effect for the ensuing school year unless the teacher is notified otherwise by a specified date, and generally no reason has to be given or hearing held. This is the spring-notification type.

Generally, tenure laws specify a probationary period (three years in 32 states) before a teacher is entitled to be considered a tenure teacher; 4 states do not specify a probationary period. Tenure laws are often opposed by the public on the grounds that they tend to freeze incompetents in positions from which they cannot be dislodged. On the contrary, the intent of tenure laws is to state fair rules and due process for dismissing teachers, including notice, statement of charges, and a right to a hearing. As regards grounds for dismissal of tenure teachers, some state laws spell out the causes, while others specify only unsatisfactory service or "for cause." The most common specifications as grounds for dismissal are immorality or immoral conduct (listed in 24 tenure laws); inefficiency (listed in 16 tenure laws); insubordination (listed in 17 tenure laws); refusal to obey school laws or regulations (listed in 13 tenure laws); neglect of duty (listed in 11 tenure laws). Intemperance is specified in a number of tenure laws, and two provide for dismissal of women teachers because of marriage.

Minimum Salary Laws

A total of 35 states and Puerto Rico have, by state law or regulation, specified minimum salaries which must be paid to teachers by local school districts. These specifications vary from state to state. In 24 states, there is a minimum schedule which specifies not only the starting salary but experience steps or increments; in 10 states minimum salaries are specified according to the level of preparation of the teacher; and in 2 states only the minimum salary is prescribed. Of course, a district may offer more than the minimum; thus several of the existing laws are obsolete in terms of common practice of school districts. Of the 15 states without minimum salary laws, regulations with respect to state aid allotments accomplish the same objective in several of them.

BIBLIOGRAPHY

Armstrong, W. Earl, and T. M. Stinnett, *A Manual on Certification Requirements for School Personnel in the United States*. Washington, D.C.: National Education Association, 1962. A biennial manual, issued since 1951.

Chandler, B. J., *Education and the Teacher*. New York: Dodd, Mead & Company, 1961, 403 pp.

Edwards, Newton and Herman G. Richey, *The School in the American Social Order*. New York: Houghton Mifflin Company, 1947, 880 pp.

Gauerke, Warren E., *Legal and Ethical Responsibilities of School Personnel*. Englewood Cliffs, N.J.: Prentice-Hall, Inc., 1959, 302 pp.

Huggett, A. J., and T. M. Stinnett, *Professional Problems of Teachers*. New York: The Macmillan Company, 1956, 468 pp.

Lieberman, Myron, *Education as a Profession*. Englewood Cliffs, N.J.: Prentice-Hall, Inc., 1956, 540 pp.

National Education Association, National Commission on Teacher Education and Professional Standards, Margaret Lindsey, ed., *New Horizons in the Teaching Profession*. Washington, D.C.: The Association, 1961.

National Education Association, Research Division, *Statutory Status of Six Professions*, XVI, No. 4. Washington, D.C.: The Association, September 1938.

Silverman, Milton, "Can We Get Rid of Bad Doctors?", *The Saturday Evening Post*. August 5, 1961. pp. 19; 47–48.

Thomas, Laurence G., *et al.*, *Perspective on Teaching*. Englewood Cliffs, N.J.: Prentice-Hall, Inc., 1961, 432 pp.

Wilson, Charles H., *A Teacher Is a Person*. New York: Holt, Rinehart & Winston, Inc., 1956, 285 pp.

CHAPTER IV

Social and Economic Status

The ranking of the professions in modern society tends always to involve comparisons of status and of economic returns. Although it is a generalization to which there are exceptions, location on the status scale tends to be determined in large measure by the latter. Therefore, the major emphasis of this chapter will be upon the economic and working conditions which obtain for teachers. But the prestige position of any profession cannot be defined wholly in terms of economic factors. The indications of public recognition of the importance of a professional service are often superficial, or are obscured, and therefore misleading. For example, Elmo Roper reported in 1950 (published in *Life Magazine,* October 16, 1950) a national opinion poll on the ranking of five occupations in the order of their importance to society. First rank (by almost one-third of those interviewed) was given to teaching. In descending order the other rankings were clergymen, public officials, merchants, and lawyers.

Social Status of Teachers

The question of the social status of teachers is difficult to define precisely. The picture is extremely confused, varying from place to place according to community background and customs. The picture varies, too, with the type of teaching position. As a generalization, it appears that prestige rank in the public mind is in this order: college teacher, high school teacher, elementary school teacher. With the growth of urbanization and the consequent removal of the teacher from close, day-by-day contact with parents, the regard in which teachers are held has become increasingly difficult to pinpoint. There are, to be sure, constant pronouncements about the indispensable importance of teachers in our society, but these pronouncements find all too little substantiation in public policy. This point is underscored in the President's Commission on National Goals:

One way to discover what are considered to be important professions is to ask which professional schools receive highest priority in university planning. It would be a rare campus on which the school of education ranked first. Yet in terms of our national future, teaching is the most important.[1]

Stanley has described nine barriers to the professionalization of teaching; among them is the relatively low status accorded teachers as contrasted with that of lawyers, engineers, doctors or businessmen. "On the contrary," Stanley says, "teachers are typically regarded, at best, as inexperienced young persons, or as impractical idealists, ill-equipped to deal with the substantial realities of world affairs."[2]

Unfortunately, data on the social origins of teachers, on their socio-economic backgrounds are not extensive. Several studies have been made of given populations of teachers, but these are not definitive for the whole population. For example, analyses of the social origins of teachers in a large industrial city (Detroit) and a large state (Texas) have been reported.[3] These were sampling studies and the results inconclusive. The Detroit study reflected the great diversity in socio-economic backgrounds of teachers included in the sample. The occupational grouping of the fathers of the teachers studied showed that less than 40 per cent were in the professional and white collar group, and slightly over 40 per cent were in the skilled and unskilled labor group. The Texas study found that teachers in that state came predominantly from the middle and upper-middle class homes.

A study of the evaluation of college teaching by 800 college students in three colleges placed the work of the college professor at the top of 15 high-level occupations. The response was on the basis of rating the 15 professions in terms of their desire to enter them under ideal conditions.[4]

---

[1] John W. Gardner, "National Goals in Education," *Goals for Americans,* The Report of the President's Commission on National Goals, by the American Assembly (Englewood Cliffs, N.J.: Prentice-Hall, Inc., 1960), p. 93.

[2] William O. Stanley, "Barriers to the Professionalization of Teachers," *Social Foundations of Education,* compiled by William O. Stanley, *et al.* (New York: Holt, Rinehart and Winston, Inc., 1955), p. 591.

[3] Lindley J. Stiles, ed., *The Teacher's Role in American Society* (New York: Harper & Brothers, 1957), Chaps. 2 and 3, pp. 13–41.

[4] Donald D. O'Doud and David C. Beardslee, "The Image of the College Professor," *AAUP Bulletin,* 47, September 1961, pp. 216–21.

Mayer has summed up in severe language his evaluation of the status of teachers:

> And among 1,400,000 people [teachers in the United States] there are going to be all sorts. There are stupid teachers and brilliant teachers, motherly types, sour spinsters and sarcastic straw bosses, dedicated agitators and bedraggled timeservers . . . it is important to know that teachers all over the world are drawn mostly from the lower-middle stratum of society—from the children of farmers, skilled workers and clerks, rather than from the children of ditch diggers and doctors. Though the status of teachers is low in nearly all countries, most teachers as individuals have moved up in the social scale—and their children . . . will move up further.[5]

Perhaps, in varying degrees, the same wide-ranging statement could be made about most professions. The major difficulty in evaluating the social origins and status of teachers is the lack of comparable information regarding members of the other professions. Because of the occupational mobility of the American people, their freedom to move across social and economic class lines in search of satisfactory careers, data on social origins and class backgrounds for any one professional group can be significant only in comparison to those of other professional groups. Another means of evaluating the status of teachers is to examine the class structure within the profession itself. The teacher is generally considered to be at the bottom of this structure. By contrast, the doctor in a hospital ranks highest, yet he is not part of the administrative hierarchy. Many view this condition as the most significant indicator of the relatively low status of the teacher. We have, however, to examine this thesis more critically. Teachers are notably self-reliant and self-directing. They tend to regard themselves as in charge of their particular tasks and resist over-supervision or minute directions from higher authority. The tasks are too complex to be dictated by rules and routines. Indeed, this deep-seated conviction of the teachers helps to explain their resistance to magic formulas, miracle plans, and automation in teaching. The significance of such an individualistic approach to their professional duties can easily be underestimated in evaluating the status of teachers.

---

[5] Martin Mayer, *The Schools* (New York: Harper & Brothers, 1961), p. 19.

Economic Status of Teachers

It is extremely difficult to make precisely accurate and valid comparisons between teachers' annual earnings and those of other professional groups. There are several obvious reasons for this difficulty. The length of the working year is one. The lack of continuous data for some professional groups systematically collected and analyzed on a universal sample—data not equally available as are those for teachers—is another. Variations in the years of preparation enter into the comparisons. There is also the question of comparisons in terms of constant and current dollars. Since 1939, teachers' salaries have tended to keep ahead of the increases in the cost of living, but they are still far below the levels of remuneration of other professional groups.

Before making comparisons with other groups, the actual average annual salary of teachers and these salaries in terms of purchasing power should be examined. The word *teacher* here includes all instructional personnel.

TABLE 9

AVERAGE SALARIES OF PUBLIC SCHOOL TEACHERS AND PURCHASING
POWER OF SALARIES, BY DECADES SINCE 1920

| School Year | Average Salary for School Year | PURCHASING POWER OF SALARIES | |
		In 1947–49 Prices	In 1959–60 Prices
1920–21	$1,091	$1,369	$1,724
1930–31	1,440	2,143	2,699
1940–41	1,470	2,406	3,030
1950–51	3,126	2,876	3,620
1960–61	5,389	4,250	5,351

Source: National Education Association, Research Division, *Economic Status of Teachers in 1960–61*, Research Report 1961-R4 (Washington, D.C.: The Association, 1961), Adapted from Table 30, p. 40.

Since 1920–21, the teacher's average annual salary in terms of current dollars has gone up about five times, but in terms of purchasing power only about three times.

Another means of making a comparative analysis of the earnings of public school teachers and other groups is to assign a constant index to the former and derive relative indexes for the other groups. This is done in Table 10.

TABLE 10

Indexes of Average Annual Earnings of Selected Groups Based on Salaries of Public School Teachers, by Decades Since 1930

Year	Teachers Estimated Calendar-Year Salary	All Persons Work-ing for Wages	Employ-ees in Manu-facturing	Civilian Employ-ees of Federal Govern-ment	NONSALARIED PROFESSIONAL PRACTITIONERS		
					Dentists	Lawyers	Physicians
1930	100.0	96.0	104.4	124.1	282.1	364.5	341.8
1940	100.0	89.7	98.8	130.6	228.6	310.8	306.3
1950	100.0	98.6	108.2	114.9	243.8	273.7	404.1
1960	100.0	90.4	102.3	—	—	—	—

Source: National Education Association, Research Division, *Economic Status of Teachers in 1960–61*, Research Report 1961-R4 (Washington, D.C.: The Association, 1961), Adapted from Table 32, p. 42.

The NEA Research Division in the study cited above compared the average earnings of teachers with those of all professional, technical, and kindred workers for the year 1958 as follows:

All professional, technical and kindred workers	$5,906.00
Public school teachers (all instructional staff)	4,122.00
Educators in colleges and private schools	4,967.00
All educators (in all types of schools)	4,273.00

Comparisons with 17 Other Professions

Because about 40 per cent of the workers in occupations classed by the Census Bureau as professional, technical, and kindred work are engaged in occupations that do not require college graduation, the figures above are not too meaningful. Thus, comparisons were made with 17 professions which require the bachelor's degree or higher for admission to practice. The 17 categories of professional workers were architects, chemists, clergymen, dentists, dietitians, engineers, foresters and conservationists, lawyers and judges, librarians, natural scientists, optometrists, osteopaths, pharmacists, physicians and surgeons, social and welfare workers, social scientists, and veterinarians. The average earnings in 1958 of all workers in these fields were $8,516.00; of those with four years of college, $9,008.00; of those with five years or more of college, $10,664.00. For all public school teachers, the average earnings in 1958 were

$4,122; for those with four years of college, $3,827; and for those with five years or more of college, $5,373.

The predominance of women in teaching doubtless contributes significantly to the comparatively low earnings of the total group. Lower pay for women than for men characterizes the other professions also, but there are relatively few women in the 17 other professional groups. For example, in 1958, women constituted 70.9 per cent of all instructional personnel in the public schools, but only 8.5 per cent of the membership of the other 17 professions. Also, only 53.3 per cent of the teachers worked 48 weeks or more in 1958, whereas 92.9 per cent of the workers in the other professions did. In 1958, the average earnings of all public school teachers were only 51.1 per cent of the average earnings of the 17 other professional groups. The average earnings of women teachers in the public schools were 94.9 per cent of the average earnings of women in the other 17 professional groups. But for men teachers, average earnings were only 57.6 per cent of those of men in the other groups.

Still another significant comparison of the economic status of teachers with other professional groups is starting salaries. Endicott[6] reported average starting salaries, for men college graduates in 1961 as follows:

Field	June 1961 Graduates	June 1960 Graduates
Engineers	$6,240	$6,120
Accountants	5,496	5,352
Sales	5,412	5,280
General Business Trainees	5,268	5,136
Average All Fields	5,640	—

By comparison, the median starting salary of teachers with the bachelor's degree in 1960, in cities in the population group 30,000 to 100,000 was $4,250.

Current Salary Status of Teachers

Teachers' salaries (total instructional staff) have shown steady gains in the past decade, rising at an average annual rate of 5.6

---

[6] Frank S. Endicott, "Trends in the Employment of College and University Graduates in Business and Industry, 1961," Fifteenth Annual Report (Evanston, Illinois: Northwestern University, December 1960), p. 10.

per cent. The estimated average salary in 1960–61 ($5,389) represents an increase of 72.4 per cent over the 1950–51 average ($3,126). In terms of purchasing power, however, the gain was about 48 per cent. For classroom teachers, the estimated average salary in 1960–61 was $5,215, or 97 per cent of that of the total instructional staff; for elementary school teachers, the estimated average was $5,034, for high school teachers, $5,500. There has been a steady closing of the gap between the pay of elementary and high school teachers in the last decade. In 1950–51, elementary school teachers' average pay was about 82 per cent of that of high school teachers; in 1960–61, it was about 92 per cent. These gains for elementary school teachers reflect, of course, two basic factors: (1) the almost universal adoption of the single salary schedule; and (2) the requirement of the bachelor's degree for elementary school teachers. In 1961, only 7 states and Puerto Rico required less than college graduation for regular, initial certification for elementary school teachers. In 1950–51, only some 20 states had reached the degree minimum.

Nonwage Benefits

The so-called "fringe benefits" or nonwage benefits have come to be an important consideration in the economic status of industrial employees. Adoption of these provisions for teachers has emerged more slowly, but now appears to be on the way to becoming universal practice. However, fringe benefits for teachers have lagged even more than salary adjustments. Nonwage benefit provisions are essential to a satisfactory climate in which teachers can perform services at professional levels.

Retirement provisions. Perhaps foremost among the nonwage economic considerations which tend to increase the attractiveness of teaching as a lifetime career is that of adequate retirement plans. Presently all states have established state-wide retirement systems for public school teachers. Development of such plans is comparatively recent. Plans for municipal employees (firemen and policemen, for example) were developed much earlier. Apparently, the first retirement plan for teachers was the Old Age and Disability and Annuity Association, founded in New York City in 1887, with no support from public funds. Similar associations were subsequently established in Baltimore, Boston, Cincinnati, Philadelphia, and the District of Columbia. The first state-wide system was established in New Jersey in 1896. As a general rule, as state systems were established, the existing city systems were absorbed into the state plans, but 23 cities still have their own separate systems (Atlanta; Baltimore; Boston; Chicago; Denver; Des Moines; Detroit; District of Columbia; Duluth; Kansas City, Kansas; Kansas City, Missouri; Knoxville; Los Angeles; Memphis; Milwaukee; Minneapolis; New Orleans; New York; Omaha; St. Louis; St. Paul; San Francisco; Wilmington). For the most part, state retirement systems have been developed since 1930; there were only 22 state systems in that year.

Amendments to the Federal Social Security Law in 1950 and 1954 made it possible for states to combine their retirement benefits with those of social security. In 1961, a total of 38 states have made it possible for their teachers to benefit from both systems.

Provisions of state retirement systems. The provisions of the state retirement systems vary widely. Virtually all specify a minimum age of retirement. Age 60 is the typical minimum age; some specify 65; and some permit retirement with benefits at 50 or 55; and some permit retirement at any age upon completion of a specified number of years of teaching service. Also, some permit retirement below the specified minimum age for full benefits by providing a percentage reduction in the full benefits for each year below the minimum years of service. Many states also specify a maximum age beyond which the teacher cannot serve; it is usually 70. Most systems provide optional benefits by which the retiree can draw benefits during his lifetime, or may elect to draw reduced benefits which continue to accrue to his beneficiary.

The benefits provided by state teacher retirement systems also vary widely. It is impossible to pick a typical example. Below is given the schedule of benefits of one of the more liberal systems. The benefits are calculated on the basis of .02 times the average annual salary for the 10 highest of the last 15 years of service times the number of years of service.

Retirement systems are, of course, financed jointly by the employer and the employee. Teachers usually contribute four or five per cent of their salary, which is segregated in their individual accounts. This account earns interest, and should the teacher leave

TABLE 11

MONTHLY BENEFITS IN A STATE TEACHER RETIREMENT SYSTEM,
BASED UPON VARIABLE SALARY AND SERVICE FACTORS

Average Annual Salary (Average of highest 10 years)	MONTHLY BENEFITS ACCORDING TO AGE AND YEARS OF SERVICE		
	Age 60 (20 years of service)	Age 62 (38 years of service)	Age 65 (41 years of service)
$2400	$ 80.00	$152.00	$164.00
4200	140.00	266.00	287.00
4800	160.00	304.00	328.00
6000	200.00	380.00	410.00
7200	240.00	456.00	492.00
7800	260.00	494.00	533.00

the system the amount paid in plus interest may be withdrawn, or if the teacher dies the amount paid in plus interest are payable to the designated beneficiary. One of the great handicaps is that no workable, universal plan for providing for reciprocity among state retirement systems has been developed. This acts either to limit teachers moving across state lines or, if they do move, to decrease seriously their retirement benefits.

One advantage accruing to teachers in states whose retirement systems are integrated with social security is that the benefits of the latter are not affected by transfer to other states. Social security has no compulsory retirement age, but one can retire at 65 with full benefits and at age 62 with reduced benefits. Also, only 16 state retirement systems provide the benefits for survivors which social security does.

The social security benefits under the amended act of 1961, which are available to teachers in states where retirement systems are combined with social security (in addition to state retirement system benefits) are as follows: the minimum monthly amount for any retiree at age 65 is $40 (at age 62, $35). The maximum is $127 at 65, or $101.60 at age 62. For a couple, the minimum at age 65 is $60 and the maximum is $190.50. The maximum for couples at age 65 with one or more children is $254.

Insurance for teachers. In recent years, protective services for teachers in the form of various types of group insurance have grown in popularity. Types of group insurance which are now available to teachers through their school district or their professional organizations are accident, health, hospitalization, surgical, life, and personal liability. Table 12 below lists the various types of insurance available to teachers, and the methods of cost sharing, in 426 school districts of 30,000 or more in population.

TABLE 12

TYPES OF INSURANCE PROTECTION FOR TEACHERS IN 426 SCHOOL
DISTRICTS OF 30,000 OR MORE POPULATION, 1955–56

| | | | COST BORNE BY | | |
| | | | ——(NUMBER OF SCHOOL DISTRICTS)—— | | |
Type of Insurance	No. of Districts Providing	Per Cent of Districts Providing	By Teacher Exclusively	By School District Exclusively	Shared by Teacher and School District
Accident	346	81	275	52	19
Health	353	83	337	4	12
Hospitalization	411	96	385	9	17
Surgical	371	87	349	8	14
Life	163	38	116	11	36
Liability	174	41	61	101	12
Other	72	17	18	51	2

Source: National Education Association, Research Division and American Association of School Administrators, *Insurance and Health Protection for Teachers,* Educational Research Service Circular, No. 5, 1956 (Washington, D.C.: The Association, May 1956), Table A, p. 2.

From Table 12 it is apparent that hospitalization insurance is the most frequently provided (96 per cent of the districts) but only nine districts pay the full cost. By far, the type of insurance for which districts tend to pay the full cost is personal liability against damage suits arising from pupil injuries. Nearly one-fourth of the districts bear the entire cost of this type of insurance for their teachers. In addition, most of the state education associations, to which about 92 per cent of the 1,545,549 instructional staff members of the public schools belonged in 1961, make available group insurance for their members on a voluntary basis with each member paying the cost. The types of insurance and the number of state associations providing each are: Life (24); Hospital and Surgical (29); Income Protection (32); Automobile (23); Liability (16).

The NEA also inaugurated a voluntary group term-life insurance program for its 765,616 members in 1961.

Leaves of absences. Most public school districts, nonpublic schools, and higher education institutions now have stated policies with full pay, partial pay, or no pay, for various types of teacher leaves; the most common of which are sick leave, maternity leave, professional growth leaves, and sabbatical leaves. Although some of the smaller school districts make no provision for leaves with pay because of illness, the trend is toward universal coverage in such cases. An analysis of the practices of 3,843 school districts of 2500 or more population revealed that 98 per cent provided sick leave with full pay for a specified number of days. Only 17 districts had no policy of pay for sick leave. The median number of days allowed with full salary was 10; the range was from less than 5 days to 30 or more; and about 9 of 10 districts permitted accumulation of sick leave from year to year, the range being from about 10 days to 200 or more.[7]

As a general rule, maternity leave is granted without pay, but the job rights of the absent teacher are protected. In 1955–56, 67 per cent of the districts in the study referred to above provided for maternity leave. There was a time when the employment of married women by school districts was frowned upon. Ninety-six per cent of the districts included in this study employed married women.

The practice of granting sabbatical leaves, a common practice among colleges and universities, has been growing among public school districts in recent years. A sampling study[8] revealed that three-fourths of the school districts and colleges surveyed, more than one-fifth of the state departments of education, and 12 per cent of the state education associations had provisions for sabbatical leaves. In school systems, typical pay for sabbatical leave is half salary; in colleges (71 per cent) it is full pay. The leave period is a semester or a school year.

Other types of teacher leaves and the percentages of 383 reporting urban school districts (over 30,000 in population) which provided such leaves without full loss of salary (see Table 13) are: visiting other schools (66 per cent), attending educational meetings (69 per cent), community service (33 per cent), court summons (47 per cent), jury duty (40 per cent), National Guard or reserve

[7] National Education Association, Research Division, *Teacher Personnel Practices, Urban School Districts, 1955–56,* Special Memo (Washington, D.C.: The Association, 1956), 34 pp.

[8] National Education Association, Research Division, "Sabbatical Leave Practices of Representative Educational Agencies," Research Memo 1960-22 (Washington, D.C.: The Association, July 1960), p. 53.

military duty (37 per cent), death in immediate family (94 per cent), religious holidays (36 per cent), miscellaneous reasons (19 per cent).

TABLE 13

REASONS FOR WHICH TEACHERS MAY BE ABSENT FOR SPECIFIED PERIODS
WITHOUT LOSS OF FULL PAY, IN 383 SCHOOL DISTRICTS OF OVER
30,000 POPULATION IN 1955–56

Reason for Absence	Number of Districts	Per Cent of Districts
Visiting other schools	253	66
Attending educational meetings	264	69
Community service	125	33
Court summons	181	47
Jury duty	153	40
National Guard or reserve military duty	140	37
Death in immediate family	361	94
Religious holidays	138	36
Miscellaneous reasons	72	19

Source: National Education Association, Research Division and American Association of School Administrators, *Leaves of Absence Regulations for
Teachers, 1955–56,* Educational Research Circular, No. 7, 1956 (Washington, D.C.: The Association, August 1956, p. 3, Adapted from Table B.

Credit unions. Another kind of nonwage benefit now widely provided for teachers is the credit union. The purpose of credit unions is twofold: (1) to encourage habits of savings and investment; and (2) to provide loan service to members at lower rates of interest than are usually obtainable from commercial lending agencies. Teachers may invest their savings and receive interest on them from their credit union, which provides a pool from which they and their colleagues may borrow.

In 1961 in the United States, there were credit unions in 1,173 school systems and 177 in colleges. The aggregate membership of these educational credit unions probably exceeds 750,000 teachers.

Homes for retired teachers. Still another nonwage benefit that is growing in popularity and availability for teachers is the development by local, state, and national education association groups of homes for retired teachers. While this movement is in its infancy, it is beginning to gain momentum. Increasing attention is being given to the needs of the aged (or senior citizens) because of the growing proportion of our population in the retired age brackets. Federal loans at low interest rates and certain tax exemptions have given impetus to the trend. Private agencies have acquired commercial hotels for exclusive occupation by retired people. Several large colonies, even whole cities in fact, have been built for retired people. Buildings, equipment, community shopping, and recreational facilities have been designed according to the especial needs of the retired. Teachers are now just beginning to achieve retirement benefits which enable them to be self-supporting and to afford adequate housing, on a group basis, in climates congenial to the aged. Thus, the possibility of development of retired homes or colonies for teachers on a self-supporting basis is now a reality. The appeal of the special homes or colonies for particular occupational groups arises from several considerations. The desire to be self-reliant and not to be dependent upon relatives is one; the choice of a congenial climate, another. But, perhaps most of all, the desire of people to live in retirement among kindred spirits, among people who have spent their lives in the same occupation is a compelling reason for the growing popularity of the homes. Being cut off suddenly from the daily routine of active employment comes as a great shock to most retirees, but being shut off from one's longtime associates is an even greater shock.

The National Association of Retired Teachers has developed a colony at Oja, California and a recreation center at Clearwater, Florida. Presently the capacity of both are relatively small. But doubtless other facilities will be added. A number of local teachers associations, notably Birmingham, Alabama; Portland, Oregon; Omaha, Nebraska; Burlington, Vermont; and Seattle, Washington have built homes for their retired members. Several state education associations, notably the California Teachers Association (Southern Section) and the Indiana State Teachers Association have homes for their retired members already in operation. And several states are currently developing plans for the construction of such homes.

Summary

It is well known that teachers' salaries have not kept pace with advances of those of other groups. What is not well known is that teachers have lost even more ground in the area of nonsalary or fringe benefits. Since 1930, employer payments for pension and welfare funds have increased percentagewise more than seven times as much as salaries. It is obvious that both teachers' salaries and nonwage benefits must be stepped up drastically to compete for qualified personnel.

BIBLIOGRAPHY

Chandler, B. J., *Education and the Teacher*. New York: Dodd, Mead & Company, 1961, 403 pp.

Conant, James Bryant, *Slums and Suburbs*. New York: McGraw-Hill Book Company, Inc., 1961, 147 pp.

Goals for Americans, Report of the President's Commission on National Goals. Englewood Cliffs, N.J.: Prentice-Hall, Inc., 1960, 372 pp.

Haskew, Laurence D., *This is Teaching*. Chicago: Scott, Foresman and Company, 1956, 336 pp.

Huggett, A. J. and T. M. Stinnett, *Professional Problems of Teachers*. New York: The Macmillan Company, 1956, 468 pp.

Kleinmann, Jack H., *Fringe Benefits for Public School Personnel*. New York: Bureau of Publications, Teachers College, Columbia University, 1962, 178 pp.

Knight, Edgar W., *Education in the United States,* 3rd rev. ed. New York: Ginn and Company, 1951, 753 pp.

Lieberman, Myron, *The Future of Public Education*. Chicago: University of Chicago Press, 1960, 294 pp.

Mayer, Martin, *The Schools*. New York: Harper & Brothers, 1961, 446 pp.

National Education Association, Research Division, *Teacher Personnel Practices, Urban School Districts, 1955–56,* Special Memo. Washington, D.C.: The Association, 34 pp.

National Education Association, Research Division and American Association of School Administrators, *Insurance and Health Protection for Teachers,* Educational Research Service Circular, No. 5, 1956. Washington, D.C.: The Association, May 1956, 51 pp.

————, *Leaves of Absence Regulations for Teachers, 1955–56,* Educational Research Service Circular, No. 7, 1956. Washington, D.C.: The Association, August 1956, 46 pp.

National Education Association, Research Division, "Sabbatical Leave Practices of Representative Educational Agencies," Research Memo 1960-22. Washington, D.C.: The Association, July 1960 (multilithed), 53 pp.

Stanley, William O., *et al., Social Foundations of Education*. New York: Holt, Rinehart & Winston, Inc., 1956, 638 pp. See especially Section V, "Social Aspects of the Teaching Profession," pp. 577–624.

Stiles, Lindley J., ed., *The Teacher's Role in American Society,* Fourteenth Yearbook of the John Dewey Society. New York: Harper & Brothers, 1957, 298 pp.

Wilson, Charles H., *A Teacher is a Person*. New York: Holt, Rinehart & Winston, Inc., 1956, 285 pp.

CHAPTER V

Professional Organizations

A distinctive mark of all professions is the formation and maintenance of an all-inclusive association for their members. This tendency to band together probably arose out of the guild system of the Middle Ages, which assumed the responsibility not only for the preparation of members, but for their welfare as well.

The basic function of any profession is to provide the specialized service which society has entrusted to it at the highest possible levels of competence. To perform this function, it is essential that the group join in a professional association in order to exercise some controls over preparation and admission, to exchange knowledge and experience among practitioners, to protect society from incompetents, to shield its members from competition of the unqualified, and to elevate the character and service of the profession.

Thus, a general association is basic, and specialized associations within the framework of the general association are essential to professional growth.

Number and Scope of Teachers' Professional Organizations

Teaching is not only the largest of all professions in terms of the numbers of members engaged in practice, but it also is the largest in terms of the numbers of professional associations to which its members belong. No other profession compares with teaching in the number of professional organizations supported by it. Probably teachers' organizations outnumber those of all other professions combined.

The *Education Directory*[1] published annually by the U.S. Office of Education, reports that there are more than 1,300 educational associations of one kind or another. It is true that some of them are not individual membership organizations. Some are honor or recognition societies; some are educational foundations; some are institu-

---

[1] Office of Education, U.S. Department of Health, Education, and Welfare, *Education Associations, Education Directory*, 1960–61, Part 4 (Washington, D.C.: Government Printing Office, 1961, 128 pp.

tional membership bodies; and some are international bodies, but at least 1,000 are individual membership organizations for teachers. This number does not include the vast number of local associations, the exact number of which is not known. About 7,500 local education associations are affiliated with the National Education Association. Table 14 indicates the numbers and categories of educational associations.

TABLE 14

NUMBERS AND CLASSIFICATIONS OF EDUCATION
ASSOCIATIONS, 1959–60

Classification	Number of Associations
National and Regional Associations	552
National College Professional Fraternities Honor and Recognition Societies	152
All-inclusive State Education Associations	62
Other State-wide Associations (usually affiliated with state education associations)	461
National and Regional Foundations (primarily educational in purpose)	71
Religious Education Associations	14
International Education Associations	40
Total	1,352

Source: Office of Education, U.S. Department of Health, Education, and Welfare, *Education Associations, Education Directory*, 1960–61, Part 4 (Washington, D.C.: Government Printing Office, 1961, 128 pp.

The teaching profession is unique in that there is no one all-inclusive, general association at the national level to which all teachers belong or acknowledge. Perhaps none of the professions has a national association to which all members belong, but all have one such association which all members recognize and accept as the association of the profession. For teachers, there are many competing organizations. This fragmentation arises in part from the great numbers of specialties in teaching, in terms of teaching levels (elementary, high school and college) and of teaching fields; and in part from the status classifications which adhere to the different specialties. There are, of course, specialties in all professions, some with greater prestige than others. But all members of the other professions manage to cluster around the common objectives and accept a common general association, with subdivisions or separate organizations catering to the interests of the several clusters of specialists.

For public school teachers, the National Education Association comes closest to being the acknowledged all-inclusive national professional organization. But its membership (763,000 in 1960–61) is only about 50 per cent of the teachers employed in the public schools; and probably fewer than 10 per cent of college teachers belong to the NEA. There is keen competition for national affiliation in terms of the total teaching profession. The American Federation of Teachers is one competing group (estimated membership in 1959–60 of about 60,000). The American Association of University Professors (membership in 1959–60 of 42,000) is another. And the many national associations of the specialties (teaching field or subject areas) constitute another, although these are limited membership associations. The association with the largest membership, and which most nearly approaches the ideal of the all-inclusive organization, is the state education association. The 64 state education associations include in their combined memberships more than 90 per cent of the employed public school personnel. The NEA and its affiliated 64 state education associations encompass in their memberships 9 in 10 of all public school teachers and can be validly considered the unified voice of this group.

If the memberships of the specialized departments affiliated with the NEA (about 340,000 in 1960–61) were added to that of the NEA, the combined membership would be more than 1,200,000 or about 80 per cent of the public school personnel in the United States. But there are, of course, many duplications in the two types of membership, although it is not mandatory for members of NEA departments to be members of NEA. A need for a universally accepted organization obtains also for college teachers. In 1960, the membership of the American Association of University Professors was 42,000 out of an estimated total of from 300,000 to 350,000 professional personnel employed in higher education. The largest of the specialized associations for public school teachers is the Association for Childhood Education International (membership 90,000); and among the NEA departments the Music Educators National Conference (membership 34,211) and the National Retired Teachers Association (membership 175,000). Among the specialized college associations, the largest is the aggregate membership of the 30 societies of the American Council of Learned Societies (a total membership of 76,997), with the largest of the constituent societies being the American Economics Association (membership 14,018).

Table 18 indicates the extent of known membership in teachers professional organizations. It should be noted that the total membership in this table probably is not more than one-third to one-half of the numbers of teachers who belong to professional associations, since the membership of the 461 state-wide associations affiliated with state education associations and that of the thousands of local education associations are not included. No membership data are available for these associations. Considering duplications in membership among the organizations, it seems reasonable to estimate that almost every person engaged in teaching in the United States belongs to one or more professional associations, and that the typical public school teacher belongs to three general associations (local education association, state education association, and the National Education Association) and to at least one specialized association, either state or national.

The typical college teacher, apparently, belongs to no all-inclusive association (since the combined membership of the AAUP and the Association for Higher Education of the NEA aggregate only from one-fifth to one-sixth of all college teachers) but belongs to one specialized association.

TABLE 15

ACTUAL AND ESTIMATED MEMBERSHIPS OF MAJOR PROFESSIONAL
ASSOCIATIONS OF TEACHERS, 1959–60

Professional Association	*1959–60 Membership*
American Association for the Advancement of Science (18 sections)	60,168
American Association of University Professors	42,000
American Federation of Teachers	60,000*
Association for Childhood Education International	90,000
Constituent Societies (30) of the American Council of Learned Societies	76,997
Independent Departments, Affiliated with the NEA	338,871
National Council of Teachers of English	30,591
National Education Association	713,994
Phi Delta Kappa	90,000
Sixty-four State Education Association	1,317,696

* Estimate

Source: Official publications of the above organizations.

General Associations

State education associations. The 64 state education associations affiliated with the NEA have perhaps contributed more to the development of the American system of free, universal, public education than any other organized influence. Since education is a state responsibility, it is within the respective states that legislation must be sought for improvement of the schools and of teacher welfare. The associations have been the leaders in the effort to increase financial support for the schools, in upgrading standards for admission to teaching, in securing legislation protecting teachers and fair treatment for them, in securing larger and more effective school districts, and in equalizing educational opportunities.

Alabama had the first formally organized (1840) state education association (reorganized in 1856). The New York State Association (now New York State Teachers Association) is the oldest state organization in continuous existence. Eighteen of these state associations were in existence when the NEA was founded in 1857. Presently, there are associations in all 50 states (with two associations in 12 states), in the District of Columbia and Puerto Rico. In addition, there is an Overseas Education Association, affiliated with the NEA, which includes teachers in the dependent schools maintained in foreign countries for American children of military personnel.

National All-Inclusive Associations

The three national associations for teachers are the American Association of University Professors, the American Federation of Teachers, and the National Education Association. The first is the general association for college teachers; the last two cater largely to public school personnel, although membership is also open to college people. Of the three, only the NEA is all-inclusive, since all professional school personnel may join. The AAUP membership is restricted to college teachers, and the AFT bars administrators from membership. The NEA Department of Classroom Teachers is, also, a general association for teachers only, but it serves only NEA members. No dues beyond the NEA membership fee are required, and any classroom teacher who belongs to the NEA is considered an automatic member of the DCT. On this basis, the DCT estimates that about 85 per cent of the NEA membership is eligible for its services.

The NEA Department of Kindergarten-Primary-Elementary Education could also be considered as a general education for teachers of these school levels. In like manner, the Association for Childhood Education International is a general association of teachers working in early childhood education. A brief description of these general associations is given below.

The National Education Association. The NEA is the only truly all-inclusive professional organization for members of the teaching profession. Its membership is open to teachers, administrators, and special-school-service personnel at all school levels, in all types of schools—public and private, early childhood schools, elementary schools, secondary schools, colleges and universities, as well as to professional personnel of governmental education agencies, education associations, and of private or commercial education agencies.

The growth of the National Teachers Association was slow. In 1870, the National Association of School Superintendents (now AASA, an NEA department) and the American Normal School Association (now AACTE, another NEA department) merged with the National Teachers Association to form the National Education Association in 1870. In 1906, the NEA was chartered by an Act of Congress; its name was changed to the National Education Association of the United States; and a twofold purpose was set forth in the Charter: (1) to elevate the character and advance the interests of the profession of teaching; and (2) to promote the cause of education in the United States. Until 1866, when women were admitted to membership, the NEA was strictly a man's organization, dominated by school administrators and college personnel. In fact, it continued to be dominated by them until the second decade of this century. In 1920, the NEA was reorganized along more democratic lines to open membership to all teachers. The Representative Assembly was created and provided representation from affiliated local and state associations on the basis of membership. So drastic a change in structure involved some bitterness on the part of the "Old Guard" which had dominated the organization from its inception. But the reorganization came as a result of natural pressures, new problems, and the aspirations of the rank and file of teachers to achieve better salaries and working conditions, demands with which the then established leadership appeared unequipped to deal.

Perhaps the most impressive change has been that of the NEA's membership growth. Table 16 reflects this growth by decade.

TABLE 16

MEMBERSHIP OF THE NATIONAL EDUCATION ASSOCIATION
BY DECADES, 1870–1960

Year	NEA Membership	Year	NEA Membership
1870	170	1920	52,850
1880	354	1930	216,188
1890	5,474	1940	203,424
1900	2,332	1950	453,797
1910	6,909	1960	713,994

Source: National Education Association, *Handbook for Local, State, and National Associations, 1961–62* (Washington, D.C.: The Association, 1961), p. 318.

Effective in 1964, all new applicants for membership in the NEA must have completed at least the bachelor's degree.

In 1962, the NEA had a membership of about 815,000. It and its affiliated departments employ about 1,000 persons. The NEA Representative Assembly, which meets annually the last week in June, consists of about 6,000 delegates.

Structure of the NEA. The legislative or policy-making body is the Representative Assembly. The governing bodies are the Board of Directors, the Executive Committee, and the Board of Trustees.

The structure of the NEA consists of 73 units as follows: 13 headquarters divisions, 33 departments, 26 committees and commissions, and one council. The divisions are permanent organizations with full-time staffs and are financed by the NEA.

The departments (with two exceptions) are independent units, supported by the dues of their members and having their elected executive committees or governing boards. The two dependent departments—dependent in the sense that they are supported wholly by NEA appropriations—are the Association for Higher Education and the Department of Classroom Teachers. They, too, have elected policy-making executive committees. Several of the other departments receive some financial assistance from the NEA, but are supported largely by the dues of their members. Except for the two dependent departments, only the members of the executive committees of the departments are required to be NEA members. Departments are created by the NEA Representative Assembly to serve some special phase of educational interest or concern.

Committees and commissions are also created by the Representative Assembly to perform specified tasks. In general, commissions are permanent organizations with full-time staffs, while committees are not necessarily permanent in nature and some do not have staffs.

Services of the NEA. The services provided by the NEA for its membership are far-ranging, and difficult to describe in general terms. One of its two major functions, as listed in the Charter granted by Congress, is "to promote the cause of education in the United States." Although no precise data are available, it is likely that the NEA devotes the major part of its resources to this objective. Its Research Division provides the profession and public with up-to-date information on every phase of education. The Division of Legislation and Federal Relations and the Legislative Commission concentrate upon securing federal legislation to advance the cause of education and to defeat proposed legislation deemed unfavorable to educational progress. The Press and Radio Division directs information about the schools to the public, through the press, periodicals, radio and television. It produces an annual series of films on school problems and procedures, which are shown by virtually all television stations. In fact, practically every unit of the NEA devotes much of its time and resources to extending educational opportunity and to the upgrading of the quality of education.

In the second of its major functions—"to elevate the character and advance the interests of the profession of teaching"—the NEA operates on a broad front. The National Commission on Teacher Education and Professional Standards works to raise standards of preparation and certification to recognized professional levels. The Department of Classroom Teachers seeks to upgrade the conditions of work for teachers, and to involve every classroom teacher in professional growth programs. The National Commission on Professional Rights and Responsibilities seeks to protect schools from unfair attacks and teachers from unjust treatment or dismissal, as well as the disciplining of members for incompetent or unethical practices. It seeks to stimulate enactment of tenure laws. The Committee on Professional Ethics seeks to establish one, universally accepted code of ethics for the profession; it issues periodic interpretations of the various sections of the code. The Salary Consultant Service is provided state and local education associations in the attempt to secure the adoption of adequate salary schedules, either by state law, by state appropriation, or by local school board policies; and a National Salary School is conducted annually. Consultative services are also provided in other areas of teacher welfare. In 1961, the NEA inaugurated a term-life insurance program for its members. Its joint National Council on Teacher Retirement seeks to cover every teacher with adequate retirement plans. The National Retired Teachers Association serves retired members in the areas of insurance, medical and hospital coverage, and homes for retired teachers. The Citizenship Committee seeks to encourage teachers to exercise their full rights as citizens, both as voters and as holders of public office. The Division of Travel Service conducts organized educational tours for teachers in all parts of the world. The NEA's joint committees (with magazine publishers, American Legion, National School Board Association, National Congress of Parents and Teachers, Textbook Publishers, the American Medical Association, and the American Library Association) are all aimed at cooperative approaches to the improvement of schools and school services.

Professional growth. A major aspect of the services of the NEA and its affiliated departments assisting the continuous in-service growth of teachers. In general, the departments are special interest associations; that is, they serve to improve the quality of performance in the specialized teaching areas, or subjects of their particular memberships. All of these departments hold annual regional or national meetings, or both, the basic purpose of which is the exchange of ideas regarding content and teaching procedures in their specialized fields. In this sense, the NEA is a huge university aiding the constant growth of its members in the disciplines and in methodology.

It is this function of professional growth that contributes largely to making the NEA the largest educational publishing establishment in the world. Its units publish more than a score of professional journals, and about 300 other publications—books, periodicals, newsletters, research bulletins, memos, and abstracts.

The American Federation of Teachers. Organized in 1916, the AFT is an affiliated, international union of the American Federation of Labor–Congress of Industrial Organization. The AFT consists of a state federation in most of the states and about 450 locals throughout the United States. The locals are affiliated with their local and state labor organizations. A minimum of 7 teachers (public school or college) is needed to form a local. Dues are determined by each local federation, but must include local, state, and national affiliation. National dues (currently 67 cents per month) entitle members to affiliation with AFT (and AFL–CIO) and to receive the *American Teacher* magazine and the *American Teacher* newspaper. The current membership of AFT is estimated at approximately 61,000, about 4 per cent of the instructional staff of the public schools.

The 1961 membership of the AFT included 433 locals in 38 states, and the District of Columbia and the Canal Zone. The largest state membership was that of Illinois, with 58 locals and 12,676 members. Other states with membership in excess of 4,000 were: Michigan (6,696), New York (6,643), Minnesota (5,390), California (4,128), and Ohio (4,412). The cities with the largest AFT memberships were: Chicago (7,524), New York (5,208), Detroit (2,806), Los Angeles (2,186), and Cleveland (2,124).

The Annual Convention is the governing body of the AFT. Each affiliated local is entitled to one delegate up to 25 members, one delegate for each additional 25 members up to 500; one delegate for each 50 members beyond 500 up to 1,000; and one delegate for each 100 members beyond 1,000. The Executive Council, consisting of the president, who is a full-time employee, and 16 vice presidents, is the administrative body. The president and vice presidents are elected by the Convention for 2-year terms.

The goals of the AFT as set forth in Article II of its Constitution are:

1. To bring associations of teachers into relations of mutual assistance and cooperation.
2. To obtain for teachers all the rights to which they are entitled.
3. To raise the standards of the teaching profession by securing the conditions essential to the best professional service.

4. To promote such democratization of the schools as will enable them better to equip their pupils to take their places in the industrial, social, and political life of the community.

5. To promote the welfare of the children of the nation by providing progressively better educational opportunity for all.

The AFT is also on record in support of federal aid to education for school construction, teachers' salaries, and scholarships and of adequate state aid to education, teacher tenure laws, compulsory school attendance, and free textbooks.

Structure of the AFT. One of the major differences between the AFT and the NEA is in the matter of eligible membership. The AFT contends that inclusion of school superintendents would create a "company union," that teachers would be afraid to oppose administrators if they belonged to the same organization. Provision is made for membership of other administrative and supervisory personnel (associations of public school principals, assistants to principals, heads of departments, and other supervisory personnel) except superintendents. College administrators are also excluded. The NEA, as has been stated, embraces all professional school personnel in its membership. The salary and teacher welfare policies of the AFT and NEA closely parallel each other except in the areas of collective bargaining.

Even in the matter of procedure for fixing salaries, the AFT and NEA are not as far apart as they are generally believed to be. The AFT advocates "collective bargaining," a term that has come to be associated with organized labor and ingrained in law. The NEA advocates representative negotiations—the right of teachers to discuss with and make proposals to local school boards regarding salaries. It does not advocate the use of strikes or picket lines, but of negotiation and the seeking of agreements. Its 1961 resolution advocates mediation in case of an impasse. Collective bargaining means designation of a bargaining agent to represent the workers—in labor terms, the union. And collective bargaining, again in labor terms, requires a weapon or threat to enforce the demands of the workers—the strike. Yet, neither the AFT nor the NEA advocate strikes by teachers. In fact, the AFT has had a strong "no-strike" clause in its constitution for many years. The NEA had no formal "no-strike" resolution in its official statements until 1961, because it never considered it necessary to state the obvious. It has ad-

vocated professional means for settling salary disputes. The 1961
NEA Representative Assembly, in restating its advocacy of the
policy of representative negotiations, included a no-strike statement,
as follows:

> Since boards of education and the teaching profession have the
> same ultimate aim of providing the best possible educational op-
> portunity for children and youth, relationships must be established
> which are based upon this community of interest and the concept of
> education as both a public trust and a professional calling.
>
> Recognizing both the legal authority of boards of education and
> the educational competencies of the teaching profession, the two
> groups should view the consideration of matters of mutual concern
> as a joint responsibility.
>
> The National Education Association believes, therefore, that
> professional education associations should be accorded the right,
> through democratically selected representatives using appropriate
> professional channels, to participate in the determination of policies
> of common concern including salary and other conditions for pro-
> fessional service.
>
> *The seeking of consensus and mutual agreement on a professional
> basis should preclude the arbitrary exercise of unilateral authority
> by boards of education and the use of the strike by teachers as a
> means for enforcing economic demands.*
>
> When common consent cannot be reached, the Association rec-
> ommends that a board of review consisting of members of profes-
> sional and lay groups affiliated with education should be used as the
> means of resolving extreme differences.[2]

Despite the no-strike policies of the two organizations, there
have been strikes of teachers in local associations affiliated with
both the NEA and the AFT, but these have been local actions not
sponsored by the national organizations. The most recent case was
that in New York City in November 1960, when the United Federation of Teachers, an AFT local, called a strike apparently in an
effort to force collective bargaining and the designation of itself
as the bargaining agent for New York City's 40,000 or more teachers, of which only about 5,000 belonged to the United Federation.
Strikes of public employees in New York State are prohibited by
the Condon-Wadlin Act, which provides penalties, but no effort

---

[2] National Education Association, *NEA Handbook for Local, State, and National Associations, 1961–62*, Resolution No. 17, "Teacher–Board of Education
Relationships" (Washington, D.C.: The Association, 1961), p. 62.

was made in this instance to apply them. The strike was unsuccessful in that a small proportion of the teachers walked out, school service was not seriously interrupted, the objectives of the strike had already been promised by the board if found to be legal. The strike was called off after one day, and assurances were given by labor leaders that there would be no recurrence of the use of the strike by teachers. This attempt to apply labor techniques to public school teachers probably was instrumental in the subsequent passage of an act by the New York Legislature declaring teaching to be a profession. The act provided that professional organizations of teachers may register with the Board of Regents of the State University of New York and be regulated by it, and it divorced them from regulation by the labor department.[3] But the school board did subsequently authorize, as it had promised before the strike to do if such elections were found to be legal, two elections among the city's teachers: (1) to determine whether they favored a designated bargaining agency; and, after a "yes" vote, (2) to select the bargaining agency. The UFT won the latter.

The UFT, after presenting demands for increased salary adjustments and failing to secure agreement by the Board of Education on these demands, called a strike on April 11, 1962. This time about half of the more than 40,000 teachers stayed away from their jobs. The strike lasted for only one day and was ended by a State Supreme Court injunction declaring the strike illegal and directing UFT officials to refrain from picketing. Thus, a second strike failed to accomplish directly its objectives.

What the ultimate impacts of these New York City strikes will have upon means of settling salary disputes of teachers there and elsewhere cannot be predicted. Whether professional negotiation, as advocated by the NEA, or collective bargaining, as advocated by teachers unions, will come to be predominant remains to be seen. It is apparent that teachers will become more aggressive in salary negotiation procedures.

The American Association of University Professors. This is the general association for college teachers. College administrators are eligible only for associate (nonvoting) membership. It was founded in 1915. Its membership in 1960 was 42,000, and its

---

[3] New York Laws of 1961, Chapter 417.

annual dues are $8 for those with faculty status, $3 for junior members (graduate students). The AAUP defines and defends principles relating to professional ethics, academic freedom, and tenure for college and university teachers. It works to improve faculty salaries, to encourage faculty participation in policy-making for colleges and universities, and to defend its members against unfair dismissals. The AAUP has been influential in serving as a check on arbitrary dismissals of college teachers by appointing committees to investigate such cases. After thorough investigation, the committee publishes its findings. If the college administration is judged to have dealt unfairly in a dismissal, it is placed on the censured list and so published in the *AAUP Bulletin*. This is a powerful weapon since it puts the administration in a bad light, may affect its appropriations or donations, and alerts AAUP members regarding acceptance of appointments to the institution staff. Obviously, the weakness in the armor of the AAUP is that it numbers in its membership only a small percentage of the total college teachers.

Association for Higher Education. The Association for Higher Education, an NEA department, is also a general organization for college personnel. Like its parent body, it serves all such personnel, including both teachers and administrators. Its chief function is to serve the professional growth needs of its members through annual conferences, publications, and national seminars. It serves, also, to promote the cause of higher education, and, through other NEA units, it seeks to defend its membership against unfair treatment. Its members number about half those of the AAUP. College teachers tend to join scholarly societies of their own particular disciplines, and seem unenthusiastic about general organizations.

Special Interest Associations

Special interest associations are those which are concerned with furthering the interests of teachers in a given field, school level, or discipline. They provide the means for exchange of ideas and information regarding content, teaching materials, and methodology in the specialized areas. There are many of these associations—state, regional, and national. The exact number is not known, but some indication can be inferred from the fact that there are 38 separate organizations in higher education (some of these are institutional rather than individual-membership organizations); there are 25 organizations for administrators; 23 in secondary education; 23 in guidance and placement; 22 in the social sciences; 20 for women in education; 17 in research; 16 in language arts; 16 in childhood education; 16 for librarians; 15 in journalism; 15 in physical education; 15 in teacher education; 13 in industrial arts; 13 in music; and 12 in history.

It is obvious, therefore, that only the largest of the national special interest associations can be discussed here.

Special interest associations of the NEA. There are 33 departments of the NEA, each of which represents the special interests (or teaching fields) of teachers. Special interest groups served by these departments are: health, physical education, and recreation; teacher education; school administration; school librarians; driver education; research; industrial arts; higher education; supervision and curriculum development; audio-visual instruction; classroom teachers; exceptional children; elementary, kindergarten, and nursery education; elementary school principals; foreign languages; home economics; music; art; educational secretaries; journalism; adult education; secondary school principals; deans of women; social studies; women administrators; mathematics; retired teachers; school public relations; science; rural education; speech; business education; and vocational education.

The Association for Childhood Education International. Previously, this was mentioned as a general association for teachers of a given school level. It is that, but it is more of a special interest association than a general one. It serves teachers who work with children from ages 2 to 12. Its membership is about 90,000 including about 3,000 international members. It publishes *Childhood Education,* a monthly professional journal, and many bulletins dealing with early childhood education.

National Council of Teachers of English. Membership in the NCTE is open to all persons interested in the improvement of English teaching, and is one of the few associations serving teachers in elementary and secondary schools and colleges. Its 1960 membership was 30,591 with an additional 30,754 subscribers to its 3 journals—*Elementary English* (for elementary school teachers), *English Journal* (for high school teachers), and *College English* (for college teachers). It also publishes research studies, teaching aids, and instructional material in the field. It holds an annual convention and conducts many summer workshops on college campuses.

The American Council of Learned Societies. The ACLS, organized in 1919, is a federation of 30 national scholarly societies in the humanities and the social studies. It is an institutional rather than an individual-membership organization, with its chief financial support coming from foundations. The constituent societies (with one exception) are the individual-membership bodies with some 70,000 members, mostly college teachers.

American Association for the Advancement of Science. The AAAS, founded in 1848, is the broadest special interest association in the fields of science, especially for college teachers and for those engaged in research in private industry and government. The work and membership of the AAAS cover all fields of science (18 sections); its membership in 1960 was 60,168. It is not only an individual-membership organization, but a federation of 291 scientific societies, academies (including 46 state academies of science, and other organizations). Its stated objectives are to further the work of scientists, to facilitate cooperation among scientists, to improve the effectiveness of science in the promotion of human welfare, and to increase public understanding and appreciation of the importance and promise of the methods of science in human progress. Its annual membership dues of $8.50 include a subscription to *Science,* a weekly professional journal. It publishes many volumes on science, and sponsors a science library program, which is used by about 2,000 schools.

Associations of Higher Education

The American Association of Colleges for Teacher Education. The AACTE is primarily an organization of institutional members (about 600 colleges and universities) engaged in teacher education. However, in 1958, it organized the Associated Organizations for Teacher Education which include a cluster of associations serving the special interests of individual members who are college and university staff members in the several areas of professional education. The separate associations have their own membership dues, elected officers and boards, and some maintain full-time staffs. Most hold their annual meetings in connection with that of the AACTE. The separate associations of the AOTE estimated memberships are: American Home Economics Association (26,724); American Vocational Association (30,000); Association for the Education of Teachers in Science (193); Association for Field Services in Teacher Education (45 institutional); Association for Student Teaching (3,000); Department of Audio-Visual Instruction (5,000); National Association for Business Teacher Education (276 institutional); National Institutional Teacher Placement Association (231 institutional); National Society of College Teachers of Education (500); and Philosophy of Education Society (286).

The American Council on Education. The ACE is considered the general association for colleges and universities; it has only institutional members. About 1,100 colleges and universities are members of the ACE, organized in 1918, largely to coordinate relations between the federal government and higher education institutions on matters growing out of World War I. It has continued to serve this purpose and to seek federal legislation in the interests of higher education; but it also carries on numerous studies.

Other institutional membership organizations in higher education are the Association of American Colleges (basic membership consists of private liberal arts colleges and universities and liberal arts colleges of public universities). The Association of Land Grant Colleges and State Universities is the membership organization for the 68 land grant colleges and universities; the American Association of Junior Colleges numbers in its membership about 600 public and private junior colleges; the Assocation of American Universities includes about 40 major private and public universities distinguished for their graduate and research programs.

Accrediting associations. There are six regional accrediting associations made up of voluntary associations of college and university teachers and administrators, and administrators of secondary schools. The regional associations accredit the general programs of colleges and universities and high schools. The six regional associations and the dates of their founding are: The New England Association of Colleges and Secondary Schools (1885), the Middle States Association of Colleges and Secondary Schools (1892), the North Central Association of Colleges and Secondary Schools (1895), The Northwest Association of Secondary and

Higher Schools (1918), The Southern Association of Colleges and Secondary Schools (1895), and the Western College Association (1948). In addition, there are 23 national organizations which accredit colleges and universities for preparation for the respective professions.

BIBLIOGRAPHY

American Federation of Teachers, Commission on Educational Reconstruction, *Organizing the Teaching Profession.* Glencoe, Illinois: The Free Press, 1955, 320 pp.

Huggett, A. J., and T. M. Stinnett, *Professional Problems of Teachers,* Chapter 14, "Teachers' Professional Organizations," pp. 335–82. New York: The Macmillan Company, 1956, 468 pp.

Lieberman, Myron, *Education as a Profession,* Chapter 9, "Education Associations," pp. 287–96; Chapter 10, "Teachers Unions," pp. 297–333. Englewood Cliffs, N.J.: Prentice-Hall, Inc., 1956, 540 pp.

National Education Association, *Handbook for Local, State, and National Associations, 1961–62.* Washington, D.C.: The Association, 1961, 343 pp.

Stanley, William O., *et al., The Social Foundations of Education,* "The Educational Profession and Organized Labor," pp. 615–24. New York: Holt, Rinehart & Winston, Inc., 1956, 638 pp.

Stinnett, T. M., *The Teacher and Professional Organizations,* Third Edition. Washington, D.C.: National Education Association, National Commission on Teacher Education and Professional Standards, 1956, 166 pp.

Thomas, Laurence G., *et al., Perspective on Teaching,* Part III, "Teaching as a Profession," pp. 305–417. Englewood Cliffs, N.J.: Prentice-Hall, Inc., 1961, 432 pp.

Wesley, Edgar B., *NEA: The First Hundred Years.* New York: Harper & Brothers, 1957, 419 pp.

CHAPTER VI

The Preparation of Members

Admission to practice in a profession now almost exclusively depends upon the completion of prescribed, specialized college and university courses. In addition, in most of the professions, a qualifying examination for licensure is required. The prescribed curricula are professional in nature, as contrasted with completion of general college or university degrees. Only a scattering of recognized professional occupations still permit occasional variation from this pattern, usually in the form of a combination of study, internship, and examination. These variations are aimed at exceptional cases and are so rarely used as to be insignificant.

The reasons for this universal development among the professions are many, but there are two basic ones: (1) the staggering proliferation of knowledge has simply made the casual, informal study and learning-on-the-job approach obsolete; and (2) the complexity of society forces the assignment of highly specialized functions to expert groups or institutions. Intellectual training and testing, as measures of competence, have emerged as the distinctive characteristics of professions. An additional consideration of great importance is the relative ease of administration and the assurance of a high degree of uniformity, or evenness of preparation.

The programs of professional preparation are, thus, at the very heart of competence and professional status. Consequently, an extraordinary concern for the quality of these programs, and a zealous safeguarding of their integrity are marked in each professional group.

McGlothlin has enumerated the two basic aims of professional education: (1) providing professionally educated entrants to the professions in adequate numbers; (2) maintaining or increasing the quality of entrants to the professions to satisfy society's needs; the first aim is quantitative, the second qualitative.[1]

Haskew has identified the difference between professional edu-

---

[1] William J. McGlothlin, *Patterns of Professional Education* (New York: G. P. Putnam's Sons, 1960), pp. 2, 4.

cation and nonprofessional education as threefold. (1) Professional education does not leave to chance the cultivation of those attributes—ethics, disciplines, methods of thought, allegiances—which make the professional fit to assume the trusteeship which society entrusts him. (2) Professional education focuses upon the person as an individual who is to practice and seeks to broaden his human—that is, his mental, moral, and emotional—capacities. (3) Professional education simply cannot stop short of performance; it cannot accept without unmistakable proof the dictum that knowledge alone is power.[2]

Historical Development of Education for the Professions

The evolution of preparation for the professions was traced briefly in Chapter I. In the ancient world, formalized and professional training, as such, simply did not exist. In the Middle Ages, training through apprenticeship and admission by examination were characteristic of the guild system. The traditional designation of the ministry, law, and medicine as the "learned professions" arose because they were the first to emerge from university training.

Gradually the guilds gave way to professional associations, and the assignment of the training function to the universities followed. The adoption by the universities of the qualifying examination, on top of formal training, was an effort to raise the quality of education, and probably was borrowed from the guilds which used it to test competence of practitioners trained under the apprenticeship system.

In early America, preparation for the professions, except for the ministry, was almost entirely obtained through apprenticeship or preceptorship. The person desiring to learn a profession simply became associated with an experienced practitioner. There were no standards he had to meet. Indeed, even after professional schools were established, this practice continued and not until the early years of this century was it abandoned in most professions. Medical education as a formal process began in Philadelphia in 1765. Following the Revolutionary War, the other professions began

---

[2] L. D. Haskew, "Planning Institutional Programs," *The Education of Teachers: Considerations in Planning Institutional Programs* (Washington, D.C.: National Commission on Teacher Education and Professional Standards, National Education Association, 1960), pp. 44–47.

establishing professional schools. The University of Maryland established a law faculty in 1816; law schools were founded at Harvard in 1817, at Yale in 1824, and at the University of Virginia in 1826. In technology, the United States Military Academy, established in 1802, and Rensselaer School, founded in 1824, were the first to offer professional instruction. The Philadelphia College of Pharmacy was founded in 1821; and Baltimore College of Dental Surgery began in 1840. Rapid proliferation of professional schools occurred after the Civil War; many had low standards and operated for profit. The universities began to establish professional schools or to absorb existing proprietary schools, but not until after the beginning of the twentieth century did the movement to make professional schools of high quality gain momentum. Prior to this time, facilities were poor, staffs were inferior, and admission requirements indifferent or nonexistent.

The factors giving impetus to higher quality of professional schools were increased demands for professional services, increased wealth, expanding industry, the growth of cities, the growth of higher education and graduate institutions, and the development of professional associations and accrediting agencies. Currently, there are at least 25 well established professions with fully accredited professional schools.[3]

Origins and Development of Professional Preparation of Teachers

The concept that teachers should have specific preparation for their work probably originated from the influences of the Reformation and the rise of secular schools. Martin Luther advocated free, universal, secular schools and special training for teachers in these schools.[4] Education of teachers, however, as a specialized, professional endeavor is of comparatively recent origin. For elementary school teachers, the concept in the United States is only about a

---

[3] For a comprehensive discussion of the history of education for the professions see John S. Brubacher, "The Evolution of Professional Education," *Education for the Professions,* Sixty-First Yearbook of the National Society for the Study of Education, Part II, Chapter III (Chicago: University of Chicago Press, 1962), pp. 47–67; and Lloyd E. Blauch, ed., *Education for the Professions,* "Professional Education in the United States," Chapter 2 (Washington, D.C.: Government Printing Office, 1955), pp. 9–17.

[4] Edgar W. Knight, *Education in the United States,* 3rd rev. ed. (New York: Ginn and Company, 1951), p. 310.

century and a half old; for high school teachers, common acceptance of the idea has emerged in this century. Antedating the development in this country of special schools for this purpose were the normal schools of France and Germany, which provided the models for our first teacher education institutions.

Massachusetts did not set up a training school for teachers until almost 200 years after the adoption of the laws of 1642 and 1647 mandating the establishment of town schools. While Massachusetts did establish the first state normal school at Lexington, in 1839, there were earlier efforts to provide teacher training for the common schools. Knight lists Samuel McCorkle as probably establishing the first formal program for the education of teachers in his private Zion Parnassus Academy in North Carolina in 1785.[5]

Samuel R. Hall established in Vermont, in 1823, a private academy, which offered a three-year course for the preparation of teachers for the common schools. Private academies in New York State began offering teacher training programs as early as 1831. Governor Clinton proposed to the New York Legislature in 1826 that a state-supported school for training teachers be established. Although the legislature did not approve this proposal, preferring to leave the function to private institutions with some subsidy from the state, in 1827 it passed an act, one purpose of which was to promote the education of teachers. This was the first such act passed in a state. Not until 1844 did New York establish its first school (at Albany) specifically for the purpose of educating teachers. In Massachusetts, agitation for state schools for preparing teachers was begun by James G. Carter in the early 1820's. Carter's argument for the establishment of special schools to prepare teachers was set forth as follows:

> Our ancestors ventured to do what the world has never done before, in so perfect a manner, when they established the free schools. Let us do what they have never so well done yet, and establish an institution for the exclusive purpose of preparing instructors for them. This is only a second part, a development or consummation of the plan of our fathers.[6]

---

[5] For a detailed account of the origin and development of teacher education in the United States, see Edgar W. Knight, *op. cit.*, pp. 309, 345.

[6] James G. Carter, as quoted by R. Freeman Butts and Laurence A. Cremin, *A History of Education in American Culture* (New York: Holt, Rinehart & Winston, Inc., 1953), pp. 230–31.

Carter's efforts, along with those of Horace Mann and Charles Brooks, eventuated in the founding of the first state normal school in Lexington in 1839.

The normal school movement spread rapidly westward under the impact of the founding of public common schools and their demand for teachers, a need which private academies and colleges made little effort to meet. By 1895, there were probably as many as 350 public and private normal schools in existence.[7]

By 1890, a new trend was developing—the transformation of the normal schools into degree-granting teachers colleges. This development arose from the growing demands for advanced education, resulting in the establishment of public high schools and the rise of accrediting agencies which enforced higher preparation standards for teachers. Between 1881 and 1950, a total of 139 normal schools became state teachers colleges.[8]

By 1930, another vast transformation in the character of teacher education institutions began. This was the evolution of the single-purpose state teachers colleges into multiple-purpose general state colleges. Between 1930 and 1961, about 140 such transformations were made, leaving only 44 public and 11 private teachers colleges remaining. Meanwhile, many of the original normal schools had evolved into state universities. The single-purpose teacher education institution is clearly disappearing from the American educational scene. There are several causes involved, but the growing acceptance of education as a discipline and of teacher education as a professional process appear to be the compelling ones. A distinct unit for teacher education is now maintained by virtually all colleges and universities preparing teachers and the professional school of education is now an integral part of most universities. The trend toward making these exclusively graduate level schools is just now beginning to emerge.

The emergence of teacher education in the universities was also slow, lagging behind developments in the normal schools. As with the normal school idea, the first efforts occurred in the East, but the eastern colleges and universities, generally, were content to let the

---

[7] Newton Edwards and Herman G. Richey, *The School in the American Social Order* (Boston: Houghton Mifflin Company, 1947), p. 777.

[8] Rees H. Hughes, "Changing Status of Teacher Education Institutions," *The Journal of Teacher Education* (March 1951), pp. 48–50.

normal schools carry the load. Before sufficient normal schools could be founded in the West, the state universities were under pressures to supply teachers for the common schools. It was, therefore, in the West where the movement to establish chairs of Education or Normal Training Departments gained a solid foothold in the universities.

New York University appears to have been the first to establish a chair, in 1832, but dropped it after a few years. Likewise, Brown established a normal department in 1850, but dropped it four years later when Rhode Island established a normal school. State universities in the West instituted teacher education programs of some type as follows: Iowa (1855), Wisconsin (1856), Missouri (1868), Kansas (1876); three began such work in 1881, North Dakota, Utah, and Wyoming.

Current Status of Teacher
Education in the United States

Presently, a total of 1,150 colleges and universities are authorized to prepare teachers in the United States. Distribution of these institutions by type and control is as follows:[9]

Type of Institution	NUMBER OF INSTITUTIONS BY TYPE OF CONTROL		
	Public	Private	Total
Teachers Colleges	44	11	55
General Colleges (liberal arts colleges)	190	572	762
Universities	105	139	244
Technical Schools*	—	—	32
Junior Colleges*	—	—	51
Unclassified*	—	—	6
Totals	339	722	1,150

* Data on types of control are not available.

The latest data reflect that teachers colleges prepare about 20 per cent of our new teachers each year, the general colleges about 45 per cent, and the universities about 35 per cent. The public colleges and universities prepare about two-thirds of the teachers and the private institutions about one-third.

[9] W. Earl Armstrong and T. M. Stinnett, *A Manual on Certification Requirements for School Personnel in the United States,* 1961 ed. (Washington, D.C.: National Education Association, National Commission on Teacher Education and Professional Standards, 1962), Table 1, p. 151.

All 1,150 teacher education institutions have state approval; 1,011 are accredited by their regional accrediting associations, 363 hold accreditation by the National Council for the Accreditation of Teacher Education. Thus, 139 institutions have only state accreditation.

Evolution of types of teacher education programs. As would be expected, there are among the 1,150 institutions a variety of programs for the preparation of teachers. Actually, teacher education institutions may be grouped in three categories: the teachers colleges, the liberal arts or general colleges, and the universities. The historical backgrounds of each of the three types are so different as to influence markedly the philosophical approaches of each to the task of preparing teachers. The normal schools, forerunners of the teachers colleges, began as institutions with a specific purpose— with curricula which were patterned after the English course in the academies, mixed with methods courses, or "trade school techniques" as the critics termed them. As the normal schools were transformed into teachers colleges, the latter continued the curricula combinations of their predecessors, although gradually elevating the content in both areas to the collegiate level.

It is not surprising, therefore, that the prestige colleges and universities tended to look with disdain upon these specialized institutions. Both the liberal arts colleges and the universities came into the field of teacher education through public pressure, and generally from the philosophical viewpoint that a broad, general college education was the way to prepare teachers; that professional courses were unnecessary and a waste of time, since the practical aspects of teaching could be better learned on the job. The teachers colleges considered the education of teachers a purposeful enterprise; the liberal arts colleges and universities considered teacher education incidental, a product of a general college education with a degree as the only needed evidence of competence. The universities, generally, were more sympathetic to specific training for teachers, probably because of the existence of other professional schools on their campuses.

At the time the first normal school was founded in 1839, there were no colleges which made any direct effort to prepare teachers. True, many college graduates, especially those who had prepared for the ministry or law, drifted into teaching to supplement their meager incomes. Thus, the public common schools, forced to resort to sources outside the established colleges and universities for a supply of teachers, had to establish a new institution. In the early years of almost every profession with the exception of the original three—the "learned professions," ministry, law, and medicine—this was true. Without the development of the normal schools, and their successor institutions, it now seems clear that the dream of a system of education for all, free to all, and dedicated to advancing the general public welfare, could not have materialized. The real expansion of the comprehensive public high schools in the United States (in which the curriculum meets the needs of all students rather than simply those of the group going to college) did not get under way until the second decade of this century, largely because there was little or no attempt to prepare high school teachers apart from a general college education. Thus, until about 1920, the public high schools were college preparatory institutions for the few.

When the liberal arts colleges and universities were compelled to enter the field of teacher preparation by public pressures to improve the quality and widen the scope of high school preparation, they tended to make only token recognition of professional preparation either by offering a course or two in philosophy and psychology, or later on, grudgingly, by inserting the courses required for licensure by the state. Little or no provision was made for orientation of subject matter to teaching and for student teaching. This kind of tacked-on program for high school teachers is understandable. The normal schools were established for a specific purpose— to train elementary school teachers. They had no other functions. The liberal arts colleges and universities, on the other hand, had many other functions to perform. Therefore, the evolution of preparation programs for elementary and secondary school teachers began from vastly different philosophical roots, and this difference is still noticeable in the reluctance to provide adequate professional orientation for secondary school teachers. But there is relatively little squabbling about the necessity of such preparation for elementary school teachers. The difference in concept is usually justified on the grounds that more "methodology" is required to teach immature children in the elementary schools. The basic reason, however, is probably the origin and the history of the preparation for the two school levels.

By 1950, the two concepts had begun to merge somewhat, and the liberal arts colleges and universities had begun to develop their own programs of teacher education, rather than having them forced and determined by state certification requirements. Presently, both elementary and secondary school teachers are being prepared in all types of higher education institutions and these programs are tending to become more alike. For example, the teachers colleges are now preparing about 24 per cent of the elementary and about 18 per cent of the high school teachers; liberal arts colleges (general colleges) are preparing 43 and 45 per cent respectively; and universities, 33 and 37 per cent respectively.

Current Programs of Teacher Education

The traditional method of describing professional programs of teacher education is to classify the components as (1) general education, (2) specialized education, and (3) professional education. While these categorizations are commonly used, they are unsatisfactory by their implied compartmentalizations. Neither are the designations of the components as liberal education and technical education sufficiently definitive. The former implies a neat cluster of separate and unrelated courses. The latter implies an irrevocable dichotomy. Actually, no such separation is possible except for purposes of convenience in college catalogs to identify departments and their respective offerings. Properly conceived, these areas of knowledge, as with all knowledge possessed by an individual human being, contribute to each other and tend to become interrelated in the mind of the learner and in their orientation to the teaching process. Likewise, the alleged distinctions between liberal and technical education are misleading. The classic notion of what is liberal education or a liberal subject tends to break down under the realities of the meaning and use of knowledge. Liberal education may be utilitarian, as well as of enduring value for its own sake. Technical education may be liberal, as well as utilitarian. A liberal subject may be a professional one and vice versa.

There is no such thing as a typical program for the preparation of elementary or high school teachers. Naturally, among more than 1,100 higher education institutions engaging in teacher education, there is great diversity. However, there are many common threads. The typical program is a four-year undergraduate one, and major attention in this discussion will be given to this type. There are many four-plus-one-year types (a year of graduate work, generally completed in summer terms, while teaching full-time on the bachelor's degree). There are also a number of five-year preservice programs (notably the Master of Arts in Teaching programs), which are growing rapidly in numbers and popularity. These will be described briefly.

The four-year preservice program. Formal teacher education programs below the degree level, quite common in the past, are now almost extinct, because the degree as the minimum level of preparation is rapidly becoming the universal requirement among the states.

What should be the criteria for an acceptable degree program of teacher education? The National Council for the Accreditation of Teacher Education developed the following suggestive list.[10]

1. The curriculum for teacher education should be purposely planned.
2. Some curriculum patterns are more promising of desirable results than others.
3. All teachers should be well-educated persons.
4. The curriculum for teacher education should provide an area of subject-matter concentration for every teacher.
5. Teachers should have specific preparation for their professional responsibilities.
6. The curriculum for teacher education should include a well organized program of professional laboratory experiences.
7. The curriculum for teacher education should be attractive to capable students who seek a good basic education for themselves and an adequate preparation for a professional career.
8. The period is rapidly approaching when a minimum of five years of college preparation will be regarded as essential for all fully qualified elementary and secondary school teachers.
9. The curriculum for teacher education should result from the cooperative efforts of the total faculty.

---

[10] W. Earl Armstrong, "The Teacher Education Curriculum," *The Journal of Teacher Education,* 8 (September 1957), pp. 230–43.

As has been pointed out, there is no typical program that can be described. In an effort to obtain a profile of existing teacher education programs, the National Commission on Teacher Education and Professional Standards analyzed those offered by 294 higher education institutions accredited by the National Council for Accreditation of Teacher Education.[11] Since these institutions were preparing the preponderance of new teachers, this analysis yields a fairly accurate picture of teacher education in the United States.

The requirements of the 294 institutions in their bachelor's degree programs were: the median requirement in general education for both elementary and secondary school teachers, 46 semester hours, range 11–97; the median requirement in professional education for elementary school teachers, 34 semester hours, range 18–69; and for high school teachers, the median was 23 semester hours, range 10–51. In teaching-field or subject requirements for high school teachers, the medians ranged from 25 semester hours in foreign languages to 43 in agriculture. The great similarities and the extent of the diversities in teacher education programs are reflected in the teaching-field requirements as shown in Table 17.

Five-year programs of teacher education. The National Commission on Teacher Education and Professional Standards has recently advocated the adoption of the minimum preparation requirement of five college years for beginning teachers, in other words, a five-year preservice program of preparation.[12] This practice will take a decade or more to become common practice. In the meantime, the practice of mandating completion of the graduate year, within the span of the term of the probationary certification (usually five years), issued on the bachelor's degree for initial teaching services, will be extended. Already nine states have mandated this requirement. The trend in this four-plus-one-year pro-

---

11 "Analysis of Quantitative Requirements in Teacher Education Programs in 294 Colleges and Universities," *The Education of Teachers: Curriculum Programs,* Report of the Kansas Conference, 1959 (Washington, D.C.: National Education Association, National Commission on Teacher Education and Professional Standards, 1959), pp. 173–92. This volume also contains descriptions of the general teacher education programs of 30 major colleges and universities, and those of teaching-field programs in 12 academic and special fields.

12 Margaret Lindsey, ed., *New Horizons for the Teaching Profession* (Washington, D.C.: National Education Association, National Commission on Teacher Education and Professional Standards, 1961), 243 pp.

TABLE 17

THE MEDIAN AND RANGES OF REQUIREMENTS FOR TEACHING-FIELD MAJORS
FOR HIGH SCHOOL TEACHERS IN 294 COLLEGES AND UNIVERSITIES

	INSTITUTIONAL REQUIREMENTS	
Teaching Major	*Median*	*Range*
Agriculture	43	24–99
Art	36	12–93
Business	36	18–75
English	30	18–64
Foreign Languages	25	18–68
History	30	18–64
Home Economics	40	24–78
Industrial Arts	37	18–79
Mathematics	27	18–64
Music	40	24–79
Physical Education	34	18–99
Science	31	18–81
Social Science	35	18–62

Source: "Analysis of Quantitative Requirements in Teacher Education Programs
in 294 Colleges and Universities," *The Education of Teachers: Curriculum
Programs,* Report of the Kansas Conference, 1959 (Washington, D.C.:
National Education Association, National Commission on Teacher Education and Professional Standards, 1959), Adaptation of Table II, p. 178.

gram seems to be to plan them as five-year, sequential programs,
in which the fifth or graduate year is regarded as unfinished business. In the absence of such planning, the graduate year tends to
involve an aimless selection of courses.

The five-year preservice programs as they begin to emerge as
common practice will probably be of two general types. The first
will be the Master of Arts in Teaching program, open to suitable
candidates who have completed a liberal arts degree. The graduate
year will consist largely of professional work, including a supervised internship, and perhaps some broadening in the general
education and teaching-field areas.

The other type will provide a cluster of undergraduate pre-edu-
cation courses in the content fields, such as anthropology, human
biology, psychology, and philosophy, and some exposure to observation and student teaching. The graduate year will emphasize
depth in professional education and in the appropriate teaching
fields with perhaps half of the year being devoted to full-time teaching internship as a part of the teacher education program and
under supervision of the preparing college or university.

Experimental Five-Year Programs

The Ford Foundation, through its subsidiary, the Fund for the Advancement of Education, has since 1951 sought to influence teacher education programs to move toward concepts of higher quality by greater emphasis upon liberal education. Woodring has stated the approach of the Fund:

> The emphasis on liberal education is not to be at the expense of other necessary aspects of teacher education. The total education of teachers consists of four interrelated parts: (1) liberal education, (2) an extended knowledge of the subject area taught, (3) professional *knowledge* as distinguished from professional skills, (4) skills in managing a classroom, working with children and young people, and in the supervision of the learning process.[13]

The three basic experimental, five-year programs sponsored by the Fund and described in the publication cited above are as follows:

1. *Professional programs for liberal arts graduates.* These experimental programs were designed as fifth-year ones for liberal arts graduates with all professional courses and experiences concentrated in the graduate year. The plan provided for consolidation of existing and separate education courses into integrated seminars and for the substitution of a full-time, supervised internship for student teaching. Several variations of this basic plan were developed.

2. *Programs for older college graduates.* These programs developed out of the pressure of the teacher shortages. They were designed to test the hypothesis that there is a considerable pool of general college graduates, many of whom would enter teaching if they could combine professional orientation with actual experience teaching. Formal college courses or seminars are pursued during summer terms, the first seminar preceding the year of internship. The programs also provided for pursuing seminars during the internship year.

3. *The Master of Arts in teaching programs.* These programs were designed primarily to prepare secondary school teachers as a

---

[13] Paul Woodring, *New Directions in Teacher Education* (New York: The Fund for the Advancement of Education, 1957), p. 11.

test of the hypothesis that a unified five-year program of preparation can be planned without sharp distinctions between general and professional education. Essentially, these programs were aimed at combining the best features of the Master of Arts and Master of Education degrees, and were jointly sponsored and planned by the liberal arts and education faculties. As a general rule, the programs were based upon the undergraduate years being devoted largely or altogether to the liberal arts with the opportunity in some cases to pursue a few professional courses. The graduate year provided for further concentration in an academic area and essential professional preparation and teaching.

Two plans have been developed in the graduate year at Harvard leading to the M.A.T. degree. The first is an apprenticeship program without pay. The first semester of the graduate year is devoted to formal course work and observation in nearby high schools. During the second semester the student is an apprentice teacher in the morning and pursues course work on campus in the afternoon.

The second plan provides for a half year of full-time, paid internship under supervision. Two interns are paired to fill the teaching job for the school, and alternate between full-time teaching one semester, and course work on campus in the other semester.

Preparation of Special-School-Service Personnel

The trend is well underway to require preparation programs of six college years for special-school-service (noninstructional) personnel. Included in this category are superintendents of schools, school principals, supervisors, counselors, and curriculum directors. This trend is especially pronounced for school superintendents and will eventually result in the doctor's degree being commonly mandated or accepted as the requirement for this position.

Preparation of college teachers. Since this discussion should cover the range of preparation programs for teachers, it necessarily must include some discussion of how college teachers are prepared. It is fair to say that there is relatively little emphasis upon what has commonly been referred to as "professional" in programs for the preparation of college teachers. Actually, there is little distinction between the preparation of college teachers and that of any other person pursuing graduate degrees. The typical regime followed by the prospective college teacher is completion of a liberal arts degree in the undergraduate college with major concentration in the field or subject of interest. Normally, about half of this degree curriculum consists of general education, the remainder of specialization in the chosen field. In the graduate school, the tempo of specialization is stepped up, so that upon completion of the master's and doctor's degrees, there is a relatively high degree of mastery of an academic field or subject. Many graduate schools do make sustained efforts to orient the specialization to teaching, and some require a practicum in teaching through observation and teaching fellowships. Also, some graduate schools require a few basic professional courses. In recent years, there have been growing demands for greater emphasis on orientation to the teaching function in the graduate programs of prospective college teachers. Although there is some evidence that graduate schools are moving in this direction, it is not as yet pronounced. There is, it appears, a general recognition of the need. One of the chief resistances to providing greater emphasis upon orientation to teaching in the preparation of college teachers probably arises from the fear that graduate schools would lose control of such programs to schools of education.

Accreditation of Teacher Education

There are three inseparable aspects of assuring a flow of competent practitioners into a profession. These are high quality preparing programs, accreditation of these programs, and the licensure of graduates.

Prior to 1927, there were virtually no provisions for accreditation of teacher education as a professional process. State approval and regional association accreditation were based almost entirely upon the general quality of a college with enough courses in education included to satisfy state requirements. The American Association of Teachers Colleges developed standards for accrediting institutions for teacher education in 1923, and began accrediting in 1927. The AATC and its successor the American Association of Colleges for Teacher Education (AACTE) carried on national accrediting in the field until 1952, when this function was assumed by the National Council for the Accreditation of Teacher Education.

The founding of the NCATE became necessary because its predecessors were not able to secure participation of colleges in sufficient numbers to be effective, or to attract vigorous support of the profession. The NCATE is a joint council of 19 members, representing the major segments of the teaching profession, including elementary and secondary school teachers, administrators, colleges of all types, the state education associations, the state education legal authorities, and the National School Boards Association. Presently, NCATE has accredited close to 400 institutions which prepare about 75 per cent of the new teachers graduated each year. Some 25 state departments of education have established reciprocity in teacher certification based on NCATE accreditation. Thus, teaching has at long last joined the other major professions in establishing a national professional accrediting process.

A Forward Look

Perhaps the single greatest need of teaching—to achieve recognized professional status—depends upon raising minimum preparation levels to those of the other professions. This movement is underway with goals of five years preservice preparation for classroom teachers for elementary and secondary school teachers, and of six years for special-school-service personnel. These plans are generally endorsed by the profession and have been implemented already in some states. In addition to extending the years of preparation, there are equally important goals of achieving more rigorous and selective admission requirements and of improving the quality of the preparing programs. The fact that responsibility for a good teacher education program is being assumed by the entire faculties of colleges and universities, rather than simply by the education or teacher training departments, indicates that the job of providing teachers has been accepted by the higher education institutions as an endeavor of first importance.

BIBLIOGRAPHY

Armstrong, W. Earl, and T. M. Stinnett, *A Manual on Certification Requirements for School Personnel in the United States*, 1961 ed. Washington, D.C.: National Education Association, National Commission on Teacher Education and Professional Standards, 1962, 219 pp.

Brubacher, John S., "The Evolution of Professional Education," *Education for the Professions,* pp. 47–67, Sixty-First Yearbook of the National Society for the Study of Education, Part II, Chapter III. Chicago: University of Chicago Press, 1962.

Blouch, Lloyd E., ed., *Education for the Professions,* Office of Education, U.S. Department of Health, Education and Welfare. Washington, D.C.: Government Printing Office, 1955, 317 pp.

Carr-Saunders, A. M., and P. A. Wilson, *The Professions.* Oxford: The Clarendon Press, 1933, 536 pp.

Cole, Luella, *The Background for College Teaching.* New York: Farrar & Rinehart, Inc., 1940, 616 pp.

Cottrell, Donald P., ed., *Teacher Education for a Free People.* Oneonta, New York: The American Association of Colleges for Teacher Education, 1956, 415 pp.

Haskew, L. D., "Planning Institutional Programs," *The Education of Teachers: Considerations in Planning Institutional Programs,* pp. 44–47. Washington, D.C.: National Education Association, National Commission on Teacher Education and Professional Standards, 1960, 130 pp.

Hodenfield, G. K., and T. M. Stinnett, *The Education of Teachers: Conflict and Consensus.* Englewood Cliffs, N.J.: Prentice-Hall, Inc., 1961, 177 pp.

Lieberman, Myron, *Education as a Profession.* Englewood Cliffs, N.J.: Prentice-Hall, Inc., 1956, 540 pp.

McGlothlin, William J., *Patterns of Professional Education.* New York: G. P. Putnam's Sons, 1960, 288 pp.

National Education Association, National Commission on Teacher Education and Professional Standards, *The Education of Teachers: Certification,* Report of The San Diego Conference, 1960. Washington, D.C.: The Association, 1960, 367 pp.

————, *The Education of Teachers: Curriculum Programs,* Report of the Kansas Conference, 1959. Washington, D.C.: The Association, 1959, 453 pp.

————, *The Education of Teachers: New Perspectives,* Report of the Second Bowling Green Conference, 1958. Washington, D.C.: The Association, 1958, 399 pp.

————, Margaret Lindsey, ed., *New Horizons for the Teaching Profession.* Washington, D.C.: The Association, 1961, 243 pp.

Stiles, Lindley J., et al., *Teacher Education in the United States.* New York: The Ronald Press Company, 1960, 512 pp.

Woodring, Paul, *New Directions in Teacher Education.* New York: The Fund for the Advancement of Education, 1957, 142 pp.

CHAPTER VII

Implications of the Future

The drastic changes which have occurred in the world since the end of World War II, and the new forces of scientific and political development already discernible in the future have been and will be so profound that their effects cannot be definitively foretold. It can only be said that it would be impossible to exaggerate the nature and extent of their consequences for society as a whole and education in particular. There will be more revolutionary changes in teaching and learning methods in the United States than in all its previous history. By all reckonings, teaching must become the pre-eminent profession, and this implies staggering changes in the role of the teacher, the nature and extent of his preparation, and the concept of teaching as a profession. Concomitantly, professional organizations of teachers will be compelled to shed their relatively simple functions of the past and take on broader, more complex procedural operations.

Let us examine some of the considerations which will exert powerful influences upon education and teachers.

Implications of Recent Developments

Acceleration in the increase of knowledge. President Truman's declaration, made after the first atomic bomb had been dropped on Hiroshima, in August of 1945, was an eloquent reassertion of H. G. Wells' reference to the race between education and catastrophe. The President said, "We stand at the door of destruction or upon the threshold of the greatest age of man." Implicit in this statement is a whole new galaxy of problems, developments and potentials. Hiroshima itself marked the ending of an era in human history and, of course, the beginning of a new one. The fact that, in an instant, men were able to discern this is itself a staggering portent. For throughout history the ending of an age had never before been so precipitous. These unprecedented pressures to adjust so quickly to totally new and mysterious forces place such strains upon

101

the educative process and upon the physical and psychological nature of man that it is not yet certain that the adjustments can be made in time. Norman Cousins states the dilemma in the title of his book, *Modern Man is Obsolete.*[1]

The intense nature of the stress of adaptation to new ages, born so quickly, can be sensed from a comparison with the slow tempo of the past. In his transition from a nomadic state—as a hunter of animals and a gleaner of the fruits of nature for his food—into an agricultural state, man required thousands of years. Only about 200 years ago did he bring forth the Industrial Revolution. Since 1945, he has had to find some means of accommodation to the fission, fusion, and space age. The dizzying pace reflects the accelerated rate of the accretion of new knowledge. While there is no precise means of calculating the rate of accumulation, it has been estimated that scientific knowledge is probably doubling every 15 years; that knowledge in the social sciences is probably doubling every 30 years; and that new military systems are usually obsolete in five years after their inception.

The chief implication for education is that the quality of teaching and learning must be stepped up drastically. Obsolescence alone forces education to drop the emphasis of the past upon simple knowledge and skills and increasingly concentrate upon the development of people at professional, scientific, and technical levels of competence. Professional workers were less than 5 per cent of our labor force in 1900; by 1975, it is estimated that they will constitute about 15 per cent. In 1900, unskilled laborers were about 12 per cent of our labor force; by 1975, they will probably be not more than 5 per cent.

The rate of the increase in new knowledge and the demand for more highly trained personnel have two great meanings for teachers in the future. The inservice teacher will be compelled to keep up to date with the knowledge in his field of specialization. The preservice programs, the preparation of new teachers will necessarily have to be upgraded in quality and quantity, and the period of preparation will have to be expanded materially.

The growth in populations. The impact upon education by the

---

[1] Norman Cousins, *Modern Man is Obsolete* (New York: The Viking Press), 1945, 59 pp.

growth of new knowledge is being paralleled by a concurrent development—the so-called population explosion. A capsule review of the pressures of this situation is as follows: At the beginning of the Christian era, the population of the world was about 250 million. Sixteen centuries later, at about the time of the first settlement in America, the world's population had only doubled. In the next 300 years, it quadrupled, reaching about two billion. And in the last 30 years, another billion has been added. If the present rate of growth continues, it has been estimated that by the year 2000, the world's population will reach 6 billion, and by the year 2050, 9 billion. The rate of growth is about 125,000 daily and 43 million a year, adding the equivalent in population of another United States every 4 years. In the United States alone, at the present rate of increase, we shall achieve a population of 250 million by 1980 and 600 million within a century.

It takes no expert to predict in general terms the implications of the pressures of population for education. With unprecedented increases in the number of mouths to feed, the number of bodies to clothe and shelter placed against the alarming rapidity with which the nonrenewable resources of nature are disappearing, man must create from the frontiers of his own developed mind the means of reverent husbanding of the resources that remain and the means of creating the physical necessities of survival.

New nations. The proliferation since World War II of new, independent nations, freed from colonial status, is one of the phenomena of modern times. These are largely underdeveloped nations starting to build a modern society with the ability to govern themselves and to achieve decent standards of living. Essential to the realization of the aspirations of these nations is the universal education of its peoples. This is a bootstrap operation of the highest magnitude. As a result of their colonial status, popular education has been meager; illiteracy is high; trained teachers are scarce or nonexistent among the native population. The free, developed nations like the United States have to face up to the problems of providing education for their leaders, while helping in the establishment of adequate school systems within the countries. Teachers will have to be exported to them, and personnel to staff teacher education schools will be required.

The Implications of New Pressures
on Individuals for Education

A prime concern of education throughout history, whether the informal instruction in the home and family or in formally organized schools, has been to help the individual to make adjustments to his environment. In pioneer days this was simple. The environment was the small rural community with a homogeneous population and common mores. There were overtones of relationships to larger political and economic spheres, but these were incidental and secondary. The tasks of the teacher were correspondingly simple, the inculcation of the three R's, deference to community orthodoxy in religion and conduct, and the reverent nurture of respect for the universally accepted and honored founding fathers of the country. The community itself largely imprinted what it considered the enduring values upon the child, enforced a pattern of conduct, and ingrained a work pattern that in itself was a great disciplining force against the small inroads of idleness. Such a setting is gone almost everywhere in the world, certainly everywhere in the United States. The implications of the growing complexity for education are awesome.

The individual and the culture. At no point are the demands upon education more clearly and complexly focused than the confusing, breath-taking impact of culture upon the individual. Herded together in mammoth cities, children are beset by pressures of their environment that make a satisfying adjustment of dignity and integrity almost impossible. The drive for lock step conformity by mass entertainment, modern advertising, and mass manipulation tend to destroy any sense of initiative, any sense of reward for virtue, any value for individual human personality. Dr. James B. Conant[2] has recently characterized the children in our great city slums as the nation's number-one educational problem.

These are largely children from underprivileged, deprived homes, whose meager cultural and economic backgrounds simply render them unfit for the traditional schools usually provided for them. Failures, dropouts, frustration, rebellion are common fruits of this educational problem. Dr. Conant calls it the nation's most explosive

---

[2] Dr. James B. Conant, *Slums and Suburbs* (New York: McGraw-Hill Book Company, Inc., 1961), 147 pp.

social problem. This "blackboard jungle" represents the failure of society and of the schools. The tragic feature of these failures, however, is that both society and teachers tend to play at the very human game of scapegoating, each blaming the other, with some justification on both sides. Society is guilty of neglect and indifference and is to blame if not for the creation of the problem, certainly for the tolerance of it. Schools and their teachers are guilty of an incredibly slow-paced reformation and adjustment to new needs, of reliance upon pat answers, and of acceding to the pressures of classicists for the one-track route to education.

A grim picture of this explosive situation and the peculiar tasks it poses for schools is set forth in an article on New York City's schools, but its import is applicable to almost every large metropolitan area in the United States.

> More than a million children of every station and every national background are living in that enormous arena, the metropolis of New York City. The city, which stifles thousands of them in jammed tenements and garbage-littered lots, also attempts with genuine compassion and real hope to educate them and fit them for useful, decent, even happy lives. It is not a simple or idyllic process. The classroom struggle for the minds and hearts of New York's young is as complex, as baffling and painful as the struggle for gain and survival which goes on in the perpendicular jungles of masonry outside . . . For more than a century and a half, as the catalyst in the greatest U.S. melting pot, New York's schools have been assaulted by wave on wave of immigrants from abroad and have been forced to spread their light amidst squalor, machine politics, and fogs of apathy, racial prejudice, and ignorance.[3]

A young teacher gave this account of his experience in this situation:

> Nobody warned me about a thing before I went to a near-slum district in Brooklyn. I was full of ideals . . . I learned a lot of things about teaching that aren't in the books. In a high school like ours you have a few tough ones and a few vicious ones in almost every class. They sit watching you like snakes, waiting for the first sign of weakness. It's frightening when you know that some of the boys carry switch blade knives. There's always a first test. One of them will start yelling, or singing, or jumping over chairs . . . You

---

[3] *Time Magazine,* Education Section, "Boys and Girls Together," October 19, 1953, p. 72. Copyright Time, Inc.

must remember that none of these children wants to be in school. They do not want to learn. They already belong to the streets. They know you cannot punish them physically or expell them. You must never raise your voice to them—if you argue, you are conceding their right to yell at you. You must never stand near them, never touch them—hatred for a teacher is part of their code and they must react or lose face if you do. You must never present them with ulti-matums. You must never cater to them in the slightest and never lie to them—they can sense fear or phoniness like animals. Your job is to keep them quiet while you teach those who can be taught.[4]

At the other extreme is the problem of adjusting teaching tech-niques and school organization to the children with gifts. This prob-lem is commonly oversimplified by the designation of *gifted chil-dren* which refers to those with I.Q.'s in the upper 10 to 15 per cent range, whereas the problem really is much broader when ap-plied to children who may not be endowed with extraordinary academic abilities but who may have other types of unusual po-tentials. Admittedly, the common practice of a school tempo geared to the average has failed to nurture adequately the nation's top-flight creative powers. This problem is now being attacked vigor-ously by most good-sized school districts, which hope to find the most effective procedure. Some critics of the situation advocate separate schools for children with gifts, and many private schools are seeking to attract this clientele. The separate school, insofar as the public schools are concerned, does not seem the most effective answer when all factors are considered. Under experimentation now are various plans—homogeneous grouping, the setting up of special classes in the comprehensive schools; for children with gifts; homo-geneous grouping by subjects (that is, a given child may be ex-tremely gifted and motivated in one subject but not in others, and is enrolled in an advanced class in the subject); acceleration and enrichment of curricula content for the extremely able within a normal class; and the preparation and assignment of superior teachers to special classes for children with gifts, or classes with universal preparation of such students.[5]

Perhaps above all new problems for teachers and schools in the

---

[4] *Time Magazine,* Education Section, "Boys and Girls Together," October 19, 1953, p. 72. Copyright Time, Inc.

[5] For suggested programs for gifted children, see *News of NEA's Project on the Academically Talented,* Volume I, No. 1, January–February, 1960, 24 pp.

future, resulting from the pressures of the culture upon the individual, is that epitomized by the comment of an educational philosopher that this is the only generation in human history for which the experiences of its ancestors are largely irrelevant. This statement, of course, is a summarization of the implications of new knowledge and mores and still newer ones already evident upon the horizon.

The individual and the state. The threatened inundation of man-the-individual by man-the-mass, the over-organization in society, and the pressures of conformity all of which reflect mounting stresses upon the individual by the culture are paralleled by the growth of big government. Governmental organization, structure, and procedural techniques mirror the kind of society they serve.

How to equip individuals to manage the extremely difficult business of assuring that government will reflect and be responsive to his will, has always been a concern of free education in a free society. But the task has been made immeasurably more complicated in this generation, and so far as can be discerned, the complexity will increase in the future.

Even if the world had not been dichotomized since World War I into the free and the authoritarian nations or the free and the communist nations, even if, as was then visualized, the world had been made safe for Democracy, this task for education would have been an enormous one. The very facts of the staggering growth in population, urbanization, the proliferation of gadgets, the predominance of mass media inevitably produced in the free nations gigantic governmental structures whose very size tended to remove them from meaningful responsiveness to the individual. With the intense competition which has now developed since World War II among the free nations, the communist nations, and the uncommitted nations for survival and predominance, the consequent infringement upon the rights and freedoms of the individual threaten to destroy the classic concepts of these principles. The paramount task of education is to preserve these concepts in a free society. This cannot be done without controversy, yet teachers are increasingly under attack by organized groups for even trying to analyze in the classroom the objectives and tactics of these groups.

Dealing with controversial issues in a free society means the making of value judgments, and value judgments are not neutral, not impartial. Strict neutrality of teachers could crush the hope of men for a free way of life. The current ferment in the United States, arising from the strains of intense social problems, the cold war, the upsurge of new nations, the armaments race, and government spending, is dividing our people into partisan camps, which have been defined with increasing narrowness of meaning as conservative, moderate, and liberal. These terms are being used so carelessly by irresponsible groups that their real meanings are becoming obscured. They are being loudly used to smear those whose convictions and opinions may differ by a minuscule amount from those of the adherents of the other groups. Take the term *conservative* for instance, it is used to categorize people whose viewpoints may range from the reactionary to quite generous or liberal notions of the role of government and the place of the individual in society. Or, at the presumed other extreme, the term *liberal* is being applied to a group whose viewpoint in many instances duplicates that of the conservatives. The stereotype, however, is the left-wing bleeding heart, the wild-eyed radical, the soft-on-Communism advocate.

Can the schools and their teachers ignore the threat of destruction of basic American values in such internecine warfare? Can they insulate themselves from these controversies, remain aloof and withdrawn from life all about them? What is the meaning and the role of academic freedom and responsibility, and how can it be preserved? These are key questions for teachers and schools and for the future of our society. For, abdication can have only one result in the long look—the ultimate disappearance of freedom and all its fruits.

The Implications of Automation and New Methods for Teaching

The traditional conservatism of teachers is a constant irritant to certain segments in society. In fact, all professions are criticized for this disposition, yet it is one of society's greatest protections. Carr-Saunders summarized it as follows:

> A word may be said regarding the charge of conservatism. There has been a bewildering and rapid development in the practice of medicine, accounting, engineering and other professions in recent times. Could this have come about if animosity against new methods

had been a fair description of the professional outlook? The charge is based upon a misunderstanding of the critical attitude toward suggested modifications and improvements of professional practice which is characteristic of any well-defined and well-ordered profession. It is not necessary here to dwell upon the necessity for testing, sometimes as in the field of medicine in an apparently tedious and laborious fashion, what appear to be promising new methods, and to ensure, before employing them, not only that they are in themselves what they purport to be, but also that they accord with proved and established techniques in allied fields and do not therefore in the long run accomplish more harm than good. That the public should misunderstand this so-called conservatism is inevitable. That responsible critics should speak of animosity to new methods as normal among professional men is less easy to understand.[6]

The reluctance of teachers to adopt new techniques similar to the automation processes already a part of industry has been the cause of particularly vehement criticism. The old cliché that the results of research are not evident in teaching until 30 years have elapsed has been used repeatedly in recent years. The clamor for automation, or more accurately perhaps, the clamor for wider use of technology in teaching has arisen from a number of considerations. The teacher shortages which have persisted since the start of World War II have created demands for the talents of the qualified teacher to be spread to a much larger number of children than the traditional 1–25 or 1–30 ratios. These allegedly arbitrary teacher loads have been under caustic attack in recent years. The hope to find means of stabilizing or reducing the costs of education always enters into demands for the use of technology. This motivation carries overtones of reverence for some new, acceptable version of the Lancastrian System. There are, of course, many who sincerely advocate technology in education because they are convinced that more effective, faster teaching will result.

The general reluctance or hesitancy of teachers to embrace with enthusiasm the use of teaching gadgets arises from several apprehensions. The general assumption that fear of displacement, loss of jobs, and the lessening of opportunities for advancement are the basic motivations of the teachers' reluctance contains some degree of truth but is exaggerated. Teachers, rather, fear the possible pre-

[6] A. M. Carr-Saunders, *Professions: Their Organization and Place in Society* (Oxford: The Clarendon Press, May 18, 1928), p. 20.

dominance of rote teaching through the excessive use of technological devices. They fear the possible placing of inordinate emphasis upon drill techniques and fact-hunting and mastery to the
exclusion of interpretation, value judgments, and the proving of
interrelatedness in knowledge. In other words, they fear the as-
sembly-line production of the stereotyped individual, the made-to-
order conformist, which in their conviction is the antithesis of what
the aim of education ought to be in a free society. They fear loss of
control of the curriculum, the imposing of the curriculum from
outside interests that are not altogether unselfish. The answer, of
course, is to find the golden mean between these possible extremes,
to find ways in which technology can accelerate and enrich teaching. This search is now achieving results under the careful, but
always relatively slow, method of research and trial and error
experimentation.

There seems to be little question that radical changes in teaching
techniques are already under way and that the tempo of these
changes, under the impact of changing demands upon education
and of technology, doubtless will be stepped up. The changes will
be designed to improve the effectiveness of teaching, accelerate
learning, enrich the curriculum, place greater emphasis upon independent learning by students, and to relieve the teacher of nonprofessional duties such as clerical work and playground and
lunchroom supervision.

Toward these ends, there is already extensive experimentation
under way in the use of nonprofessional helpers—teacher aides,
clerical helpers, paper readers; the use of sub-professional techni-
cians; team teaching; the ungraded elementary school; the use of
television—the closed circuit type, educational networks, and even
a six-state experiment of telecasting to all schools in these states
from an airplane; the use of films, tape recorders and teaching
machines; and a variety of experimental techniques for the gifted.[7]
Not only are these experiments a drive by sincere exponents to improve the education processes, but also a growing body of opinion
is that the real professionalization of teaching will be dependent

---

[7] For detailed discussion of these experiments, see: Arthur D. Morse, *Schools
of Tomorrow—Today* (Garden City, New York: Doubleday & Company, Inc.,
1960), p. 191; and J. Lloyd Trump and Dorsey Baynham, *Focus on Change—
Guide to Better Schools* (Chicago: Rand McNally & Company, 1961), p. 147.

upon a radical revision of the image of the teacher in the public mind. Adoption of newer, more complex and more efficient procedures, it is argued, will raise this image of the teacher from pedestrian performer to one of superb competence, working with imagination and creativeness.

Finally, with reference to the impingement of the future upon the profession of teaching, some things are abundantly clear. There is no fruitful purpose in bemoaning the growing complexity of society or indulging in nostalgic yearning for the return of simpler times. The complexity is a fact of life and the trend could only be halted or reversed by the catastrophe of a general, all-out atomic war. Complexity or organization is also a fact of life. Technology will become more complex; automation will grow in use, creating new problems in the education and re-education of people. Urbanization will continue and increasingly inundate the rural areas. Population growth will continue at an alarming rate, creating new economic and social problems, one upon the other. The trend toward specialization will continue to fragment society and minimize the possibility of educating the "whole man." Governmental organizations will tend to get bigger and to stifle the traditional forms of the rights of man. The cynical manipulation of people will tend to become more cynical and more extensive. Increasingly, the anonymity of the mob will offer a haven for the frustrated. These are trends which may not be checked by education, but may be kept within bounds to preserve human rights. Man is capable of infinite adaptiveness. Education, operating for the general welfare, is the chief adaptive weapon.

The imperatives of new times, new demands, and new visions require, however, an education of such quality as never before visualized in our history. Peter Vierick has characterized this goal of education as the search for America's third frontier:

> . . . the inner frontier, the exploration of our new Columbuses in the newly discovered continents behind the forehead. The symbols and the spokesmen of the third frontier are found in poetry, art, psychology, religion . . . the total human being . . . hungers not only for measurable facts but for unmeasurable truths. He needs the intangibles—the spiritual and aesthetic—beyond the gadget world of tangible things. In exploring that "beyond," the complete man

turns for guidance to the classic humanities and to religion. These may be flickering and fitful lamps. Yet they are the only lamps we have, once we move past the boundary of measurable facts.[8]

BIBLIOGRAPHY

Brameld, Theodore, *Toward a Reconstructed Philosophy of Education.* New York: Holt, Rinehart & Winston, Inc., 1956, 417 pp.

Carr-Saunders, A. M., and P. A. Wilson, *The Professions.* Oxford: The Clarendon Press, 1933, 536 pp.

Conant, James B., *Slums and Suburbs.* New York: McGraw-Hill Book Company, 1961, 147 pp.

Goals for Americans, Report of the President's Commission on National Goals. Englewood Cliffs, N.J.: Prentice-Hall, Inc., 1961, 372 pp.

Huxley, Aldous, *Brave New World Revisited.* New York: Harper and Brothers, 1958, 147 pp.

Lieberman, Myron, *The Future of Public Education.* Chicago: University of Chicago Press, 1960, 294 pp.

Lindsey, Margaret, ed., *New Horizons for the Teaching Profession.* Washington, D.C.: National Education Association, National Commission on Teacher Education and Professional Standards, 1961, 243 pp.

Mayer, Martin, *The Schools.* New York: Harper & Brothers, 1961, 446 pp.

Morse, Arthur D., *Schools of Tomorrow—Today!* Garden City, New York: Doubleday & Company, Inc., 1960, 191 pp.

Trump, J. Lloyd, and Dorsey Baynham, *Guide to Better Schools, Focus on Change.* Chicago: Rand McNally & Company, 1961, 147 pp.

---

[8] Peter Vierick, *The Unadjusted Man* (Boston: The Beacon Press, 1956), pp. 271, 291.

Index

A

Accreditation of teacher education, 39–40, 90, 93–94, 98–99
American Association of Colleges for Teacher Education, 81–82, 98
American Association of Teachers Colleges, 98
history, 98–99
national, 90, 94, 98
National Council for the Accreditation of Teacher Education, 93–94, 98–99
regional, 82–83, 90, 98
state, 90, 98
Accrediting associations, 40, 82–83, 90, 93–94, 98–98
American Association of Colleges for Teacher Education, 81–82, 98
American Association of Teachers Colleges, 98
National Council for the Accreditation of Teacher Education, 93–94, 98–99
regional, 82–83
American Association for the Advancement of Science, 81
American Association of Colleges for Teacher Education, 81–82, 98 (*see also* Accreditation of teacher education; Accrediting associations)
American Association of Teachers Colleges, 98 (*see also* Accreditation of teacher education; Accrediting associations)
American Association of University Professors, 68, 70, 78–79 (*see also* College teaching; Special-interest associations)
American Council on Education, 82
American Council of Learned Societies, 68, 81 (*see also* College teaching; Special-interest associations)
American Economics Association, 69
American Federation of Teachers, 31, 33, 68, 70, 75–78

American Fed. of Teachers (*cont.*)
goals, 75–76
membership, 68, 75
by states, 75
merit rating, 33
no-strike pledge, 76
policies, 76
salary schedules, 31
structure, 75–76
Associated Organizations for Teacher Education, 81 (*see also* American Association of Colleges for Teacher Education)
Association for Childhood Education International, 68, 71, 80 (*see also* Special-interest associations)
Association for Higher Education, 8–9, 69, 72, 79
teacher certification policy, 8–9 (*see also* College teaching)
Automation in teaching, 54, 109–111

B

Bachelor's degree, 25, 28, 32–33, 45–47, 57–58, 72, 94
institutional requirements for, 94
median salary of teachers with, 57
for membership in the National Education Association, 72
as minimum prerequisite to teaching, 46–47
per cent of teachers completing, 28
professions requiring, 56
in salary schedules, 32–33
states requiring for teachers certification, 45, 46 (*table*)
Bestor, Arthur, 37
Brethren of the Common Life, 13
Brooks, Charles, 88

C

Carman, Harry J., 5, 10
Carr-Saunders, A. M., 1, 2, 8, 14, 108, 109
Carter, James G., 87, 88
Certification, teacher, 8–11, 18, 39–42, 44–49, 73, 92
Association for Higher Education's statement on, 8–9